D0016545

**Damage Noted:**

Stains on corner & edges
09/30/04 y

# Hunting al Qaeda

# EDITOR'S NOTE

"Anonymous" is a composite of several members of Beast 85 who, in the interest of national security and the safety of their families, have chosen not to reveal their identities. *Hunting al Qaeda* was written with the participation of Bob Mayer, a West Point graduate, special forces veteran, and author of more than seventeen books.

# Hunting al Qaeda

## A TAKE-NO-PRISONERS ACCOUNT OF TERROR, ADVENTURE, AND DISILLUSIONMENT

## Anonymous

Foreword by Colonel Gerald Schumacher,

United States Army Special Forces (ret.)

ZENITH
PRESS

Revised and expanded English translation first published in 2005 by Zenith
Press, an imprint of MBI Publishing Company, Galtier Plaza, Suite 200, 380
Jackson Street, St. Paul, MN 55101-3885 USA

First published as *Sur les traces d'Al-Qaïda* by Alban Editions
© 2004 Bob Mayer, Adam R., and Alan H.
© 2005 English-language translation

Zenith Press titles are also available at discounts in bulk quantity for
industrial or sales-promotional use. For details write to Special Sales Manager
at MBI Publishing Company, Galtier Plaza, Suite 200, 380 Jackson Street, St.
Paul, MN 55101-3885 USA.

ISBN-13: 978-0-7603-2252-9
ISBN-10: 0-7603-2252-X

***Cover photo:*** Eastern Alliance soldiers wait on a ridge near the front line
in Tora Bora, Afghanistan, December 15, 2001. *AP/Wide World Photos,
Kevin Frayer*

Printed in the United States of America

This book is dedicated to our friend and comrade in arms, T.T. Boy.
Although you are no longer with us, you are not forgotten.

*De Oppresso Liber.*

—*"Red" and "Captain Alan"*

# CONTENTS

# FOREWORD

*Hunting al Qaeda* is a disturbing book. It will disturb a lot of people in the army, in special forces, in the intelligence community, and throughout the United States. It blows apart the myth that everything that can be done to find terrorists is being done. It hangs out a lot of dirty laundry that many of us would like to pretend isn't there. It illuminates the fact that even special forces is infected with micromanagement disease, petty infighting, and the fear of making mistakes. This is not some sanitized war story. It's the hard, ugly realities of military service, relationships between active and reserve components, and war. More than anything else, it's a story about a group of soldiers who went to fight the enemy and refused to be deprived of their due.

This team is composed of citizen-soldiers who hung up their business suits, stopped their everyday lives, left their loved ones, and went to Afghanistan, ostensibly to hunt terrorists. And they can justify their great sacrifice because they love God and they love their country. They have the training and the skills. They believe in the righteousness of their cause, and they believe that they can make a difference. In their deepest, most personal moments of reflection, these men probably imagine capturing Osama bin Laden. They intend to turn that dream into reality, and they have every right to believe that they might actually succeed. They are proud to be part of their country's quest to rid the world of the men who attacked the World Trade Center and the Pentagon. This isn't just any group of part-time soldiers. These men are U.S. Army National Guard Special Forces soldiers. They are Green Berets in every sense of the word.

What they don't know is that their biggest challenge will not be finding and destroying al Qaeda. Their biggest challenge will be finding how to work with a political/military bureaucracy that defines victory as not having any accidents, incidents, or injuries. This culture of "playing it safe" permeates much of the military, and it begins with many politicians.

Since the end of World War II, the political commitment to fight and win wars has evaporated. Politicians, lacking the courage to declare war, allow our soldiers to go into battle without the support of the people, as the framers of the Constitution had intended. So the politicians second-guess many battlefield operations. They Monday morning–quarterback military decisions, berate military accidents, and jump on the bandwagon only after success is clearly visible. The consequence is that they get what they wanted: a military that lives in fear of political backlash.

As if this weren't enough, National Guard special forces also experience discrimination at the hands of active-duty special forces units, which view them as something akin to summer help. Ironically, more than any other military career field, trained citizen-soldiers are uniquely suited for special forces missions.

Reserve-component special forces personnel can, and often do, bring exceptional civilian professional skills and insights to the unconventional warfare environment. But that's a hard pill for some to swallow, and it isn't much appreciated in rank-and-file active duty units.

In the early stages of the war in Afghanistan, special forces teams weren't as restricted as they would become later in the war. Special forces units deserve all the credit for bringing that war to a rapid and victorious conclusion. As time went on, more and more military units were sent to Afghanistan, with increasingly more chiefs and fewer Indians. As their numbers grew, more senior officers demanded accountability. More operations came under the scrutiny of higher and higher levels of command. The staggering number of officers in the war zone had to justify their contribution to the war. They had lost the initiative. They couldn't seize the moment. Their internal controls were choking the operational capabilities of the "ground truth" combatants. More and more, the Taliban became wise to the debilitating elephantitis of U.S. military operations.

Although the author never makes this allegation, it would not surprise me to learn that Donald Rumsfeld himself made *tactical* battlefield decisions. Oh, make no mistake that Mr. Rumsfeld would never actually call it a decision, but at his level it only takes a loose comment to rapidly become a commandment as it filters down the pipe. The Sec Def gets his way and has plausible deniability that he may have interfered with decisions that should have been made by a noncommissioned officer.

No one on this team of highly trained citizen-soldiers is influenced, motivated, or limited by career considerations. Hamstrung by higher headquarters-internal controls, they decide to break the "rules." They develop elaborate strategies to deceive both their chain of command and the elusive Taliban, which puts them in a pretty difficult position. If they fail, they could be killed, and bring embarrassment and humiliation to their team, the army, the National Guard, and their country. Although not stated but very clear to any professional soldier, even if they succeed, they may be subject to a court martial.

Many will appropriately ask if the ends justified the means. One can never assume that the author knew all there was to know about higher headquarters' operations. It may be—and we can only hope—that other special forces teams were executing unencumbered missions that were unknown to these men. Nor is it clear to me that these soldiers truly understood the enormous consequences of their rule-breaking strategies. Had they understood, I doubt their actions would have been any different. This team was hell-bent on hunting al Qaeda, and hunt they did.

*—Colonel Gerald Schumacher*
*United States Army Special Forces (ret)*

# PREFACE

Afghanistan has been a special forces conflict more than any other conflict in U.S. military history. Unlike other conflicts, the so-called "war on terror" isn't a war between countries or armies on clearly defined battlefields. Rather, it's a war against shadow forces, and the warriors best equipped to fight in the shadows are special operations men. This was the kind of war that Colonel Aaron Banks envisioned in 1947 when 10 men stood on Smoke Bomb Hill at Fort Bragg, North Carolina, and founded the first special forces unit.

As much as special operations forces may be unique in the military, they are still part of the bureaucracy that permeates the armed forces. Operational Detachment Alpha (ODA) 2085, call sign Beast 85 (2nd Battalion, 3rd Special Forces Group Airborne), held an advantage over the active-duty personnel because they were not part of a bureaucracy. The team members weren't concerned about politics or careers, about checking off boxes and looking good. Their lives existed outside the realm of the army. But during their time in Afghanistan they encountered commanders who were less interested in taking the war to the enemy than they were with keeping up appearances.

The directives handed down from micromanaging echelons to the citizen-soldiers of Beast 85 were interesting in the way they calculated risk, or the lack thereof. The forward operating base (FOB) was looking for the 100 percent solution that would make everyone look good. Because of this, analysis paralysis plagued FOB commanders. Indecisiveness ruled the day. So when action was needed, Beast 85 sometimes opted for the riskier 70 percent solution.

Sometimes their solution was the right one, sometimes it wasn't. Beast 85 witnessed massive aerial bombardments, including the infamous Wedding Party Massacre, the widely reported incident in which U.S. fighters were allegedly directed to bomb a compound full of civilians at a wedding on 1 July 2002. There were victories and there were fatal mistakes, and they tell it all.

Through sheer tenacity, valor, patience, and diplomacy, the citizen-soldiers of Beast 85 won the hearts and minds of countless Afghans and convinced them to surrender the handful of terrorists in their midst. Braving orders from above, Beast 85 captured the Taliban's military commander, Mullah Akhtar Osmani. They then went on to capture two other high-value targets and destroy over 79,000 pounds of weapons and ammunition, amounting to 80 percent of all weapons and ammunition found in the country during their tour of duty.

But a sour aftertaste lingers among these courageous soldiers because al Qaeda operatives were within their grasp but couldn't be arrested. In Mullah Osmani's case, he was arrested but then *ordered* released by higher authorities.

But the men of Beast 85 are not into politics. They didn't go to war for the sake of any particular president nor for the sake of the war itself. They simply answered their country's call to duty. They said goodbye to their civilian lives and willingly went into harm's way for one simple reason their love of country.

These people have a unique story to tell an exciting, thrilling, highly informative, and sobering story that's far different from what the army would have you believe. And they recognize how important it is that this generation, as well as our posterity, knows the truth as a matter of historical record. For this reason they have agreed to break the army's strict code of silence.

—*Bob Mayer, September 2004*

*from the French edition,* Sur les Traces d'Al-Qaïda

CHAPTER **1**

# ON THE MARCH

*Kandahar, Afghanistan, June 2002*
*1300 hours*

It was a problem you'd expect to torment a data entry clerk in Dubuque, not a special forces soldier in Afghanistan.

The convoy was rolling to the outer gate of Kandahar Airfield. Red had planned to plug his ground positioning receiver (GPR), or plugger, into his laptop to track their position on the Falcon View mapping software. It had worked fine when he tested it the previous day, but today his laptop confused it for a mouse.

Things were going to shit, fast. The plugger was only part of the problem.

There was Red, the navigator, the guy in front, with the 30 vehicles of the assault force at his ass, and his computer was acting up. Frank, who they called "Rock," was in the back manning the M240B machine gun, and Doc Ken was in the back seat.

John (a.k.a. "Ringo"), who drove, provided his usual words of encouragement: "Now you're fucked." He was always questioning Red's preparedness. He was like an older brother who liked to poke and prod, to get on his nerves. Red opened his mouth, then stopped. There was no point in arguing with him. Like any pesty older brother, Ringo was too good at twisting Red's words around and using them against him.

Red was losing it. He had just about dispensed with the notion that he had any control over the events in his life or on this mission. He was not looking through rose-colored glasses, only a white-hot version of reality.

It didn't help that it was the usual 110 degrees.

Here they were, their little air assault into the valley having turned into a big, conspicuous ground convoy. They might as well lay out a welcome mat to the enemy:

*Here we are, come and get our sweaty asses!*

As they approached the Afghan checkpoint where Route 4 linked the airfield to Kandahar City, Red knew he had to do something. He asked Ringo to pull over, and the entire convoy, minus the Navy SEAL platoon, pulled in behind him. The radio came alive with a frantic voice, full of stress like a panicked mother who just lost her child in a crowded grocery store. "What the hell is going on?" It was Major R.

He asked when they'd be leaving, saying that they had to go, goddammit, and now. The whole idea was silly to begin with— driving 100 kilometers to their objective, Deh Rawod, when an air assault made a hell of a lot more sense.

Red replied, in clear technical terms, that he needed to unfuck the navigation gear. With no plugger and the mission support site over 100 kilometers of very tough terrain away, this entire venture might just prove to be impossible.

Why was he leading this horseshit convoy, anyway? He felt screwed. Captain Drinkwine (not to be confused with their team leader, Captain Alan) dropped this little gem assignment on him the night before at mission support in Tarin Kowt.

Red's job was to figure out how to get the convoy 100 kilometers through Indian Country in 12 hours. As they rolled to a stop, he contemplated whether it was good or bad to be the lead vehicle. If someone were going to ambush their convoy, they would be wise to attack them in the middle. By letting the point element go by, you can destroy the unwitting guts of an enemy column before the lead ("point") vehicle can warn them of the ambush. That's Military Tactics 101.

But Red figured that since the Taliban were a bunch of screwups, ignorant of sound military tactics, they would attack the first vehicle—his.

Red's team, Beast 85, was in the first four vehicles: their two Toyota pickup trucks, one up-armored humvee, and a GMV (special forces humvee). The up-armored humvee was heavily reinforced with a totally armored shell on its frame. It was a heavy motherfucker with a large engine. As the point element, they were to seal off a "kill zone," blocking the escape routes and destroying the front and rear of a formation if the terrain favored it (naturally, they would be the first to find the land mines, too).

When it became clear that the plugger wasn't going to cooperate, they stopped the humvee on the side of the road. Red stepped out and walked past the line of other humvees and Toyota pickups to Bubble Boy's GMV. The GMV was a special forces modification of the vehicle that was designed for carrying a lot of fuel and water, gun mounts, extra battery power for multiple radios, and a DC/AC converter.

Captain Alan had a plugger. Drinkwine had one too, and Red was pretty sure Drinkwine had the waypoints programmed into it.

Red wanted to take Bubble Boy's device because it was his fault that he was in the lead, and he knew it would bother him to lose it. So he grabbed Bubble Boy's plugger, to his strong objections, and he was delighted that it was, indeed, loaded with the waypoints. Red smiled and headed back to the head of the convoy.

It was hotter than a bitch, a heat they couldn't escape. Every structure and object under that brutal, blistering sun, including Red's own body, sucked up the heat. Captain Alan was smiling at their misery. Red couldn't help laughing himself. He thought of how nice it would be to be grumbling about the heat in the comforts of an air-conditioned house or car, blowing the head off an ice-cold beer. But here they lacked A/C and, for the moment, ice-cold beer.

It was a pervasive, suffocating heat, hot enough to fry an egg. You could not escape it, and it could kill you.

Red looked back and saw the long line of vehicles behind him, and the main gate to the Kandahar Airfield complex a few hundred meters ahead. The Pashtun soldiers manning the gate were beginning to collect outside the assortment of ramshackle buildings that made up the front gate. The convoy approaching the gate was something unusual and they were curious to see what they were up to. As Red started to jam himself back into the passenger seat of their truck, Ringo was laughing at Major R., who was still freaking out over the radio.

"We're rolling," Red put out over the radio as they moved forward with Operation Full Throttle.

At the front gate they turned left up Route 4 toward Kandahar City and beyond. Red powered the plugger up and dug for his maps. He worked to make space for himself in the overpacked Toyota as they sped up over the tiny portion of the trip that was on paved roads. Next to him in the passenger seat, he had his water, rifle, body armor, food, night vision, pistol, maps, plugger, three radios, and a few hand grenades. It was too much critical gear in too small a space, packed tight as shit. He asked Doc Ken if there was any space in the back for his 5-quart water blivet. He said yes and tossed it on top of the mound of equipment in the back of the crew cab.

Ringo, Rock, Doc Ken, and Red were quiet as they drove through the line of hills that separated them from Kandahar City. Everyone was alone with their own thoughts. Red wasn't too worried about the first couple of hours of the trip through Kandahar and the north. But as they approached the first range of mountains 40 kilometers away, it was going to get dark, and they would still have a long way to go.

The maps that Red had to work from were 1:100,000-scale topological maps that were given to the Americans by the Russians shortly after their invasion. The maps hadn't done the Russians much good, and they weren't helping Red much either. A 1:100,000 map just doesn't have the detail to describe the terrain realistically, unless the terrain is flat. And the land wasn't flat at all, with the peaks of the Kuh-e-Mazar towering 10,000 feet above the city of Kandahar.

The roads on the maps were best guesses that followed historical donkey and camel routes that have crisscrossed the area for thousands of years, the motor vehicle being a relatively new and rare import to this country. These roads had never been paved or graded, or improved. They were treacherous.

Red was trying to track their route across four 12x12-inch maps in the passenger seat of the truck as it rumbled down the road toward the largest combat operation in Afghanistan in the last four months. The GPR showed him a screen with an arrow representing their 10-digit grid square displaying their position on the earth within 5 feet. It showed their current position in relation to waypoints that had been plotted based on the major points on the roads and terrain features. Transpositioning that location onto the paper map was the challenge. The ride was bumpy, it was over 120 degrees, and the dust was 6 inches deep on the roads.

Kandahar, the second-largest city in Afghanistan, was looming to their front, 15 minutes out of the gate of the airfield. Sitting among steep hills and dry plains, the city was once the capital of a vast Pashtun empire stretching from the Oxus to the Indus, and from Tibet to the Makhran. It was founded some 23 centuries ago by Alexander the Great. In the eighteenth century, it became the capital of local warlord Ahmad Shah, who went on to defeat the Moghuls and occupy their capital, Delhi, which lies almost 3,000 miles to the east. The Pashtun shared a proud history, and Kandahar was their capital.

Kandahar is dominated by Ahmad Shah's large octagon-shaped mausoleum, and by the minarets of a hundred mosques, one of which is said to hold the prophet Mohammed's cloak. It's a holy city, yet it's brown as the earth around it, dirty and poor. Most of the structures are adobe, and few have indoor plumbing. There is no running water, no garbage collection, no sanitation. Open sewage runs along the alleyways that separate the compounds in such a maze that a stranger can lose his way in less than a minute. The buildings lay in ruins that have long spread into the Pashtuns' souls.

And the cemeteries. They eat at the city, devouring its heart. Between rows of brown adobe stand huge tracts of land dedicated to the dead. Graves are made of stacks of rocks, all shaped the same. Row upon row of monotonous graves—men's graves, mostly. Afghanistan is the only country on earth where, in the 15- to 40-year-old age group, females outnumber males by a ratio of 10 to 7. It is a violent land.

As they approached the city, brick kilns fired by old car tires lined the western side of the road, pouring deep black smoke from their chimneys. The two major highways in Afghanistan, Route 4 and Route 1, intersect at Kandahar, and their route to the north was through the city.

As a rule, coalition forces didn't drive tactical vehicles through Kandahar. The Soviets had a large garrison in Kandahar in the late 1970s and early 1980s, and the governor of Kandahar province didn't want the population to think of them as another occupying force. He had asked them not to drive their vehicles through his city.

But they had business to take care of, so they came to a mutual decision: the governor could go fuck himself.

They were polite enough not to take their tactical vehicles, and instead drove their Toyotas into Kandahar. None of them had shaved since they'd landed in Afghanistan three months earlier. Red had lost over 20 pounds, and he was starting to look and feel every inch like a local gunman, except, of course, for his bright red beard and sunburned skin.

Today was the start of Operation Full Throttle, the first large-scale military operation since the Battle of Tora Bora and Operation Anaconda months before. Helmed by their military commanders, Mullah Akhtar Mohammed Osmani and Mullah Barader, the Taliban was regrouping in the mountains north of Kandahar. With Taliban leader Mullah Omar said to have relinquished direct power to his childhood friend Mullah Barader, the Taliban was expected to engage in more coordinated campaigns, including possible attacks on the Pashtuns' capital, Kandahar, as well as Afghanistan's official capital, Kabul. Mullah Omar had gone into hiding, and his whereabouts were unknown. His deputies, Mullah Barader and Mullah Osmani, were orchestrating a do-or-die fight aimed at bringing the Taliban back to power. Operation Full Throttle meant to stop him from achieving that mission.

So there they were, driving straight through this dense city (against the provincial governor's wishes), with a 30-vehicle convoy of humvees and pickup trucks bristling with machine guns and fully armed Americans. The convoy would be spread out in the city center as it encountered the compact mass of donkeys, carts, horse carriages, cars, and trucks. Taliban intelligence would report it. They might even stage an ambush.

As they made the left turn off Route 4 onto Route 1, they crossed under a set of concrete arches that served as the entrance to the city and as a military checkpoint for all vehicle traffic coming and going through the metropolis. The soldiers of Governor Shirzai never tried to stop them, but rather motioned them through, smiling and waving. Red smiled and waved back.

Operation Full Throttle was looking very much like a grand circus.

How long, Red wondered, before every warlord in the southern half of the country got a call: "Hey, keep an eye out for the large group of Americans, moving north through Kandahar, and packed to the gills. They're out for more than a day in the country, I promise you that!" Their entire progress was going to be tracked from start to finish.

Instead of an air assault on carefully specified targets, followed by a cordon of the villages and a detailed search, they were driving a huge convoy of humvees and Toyotas up into the central mountains of Pushtu country. Red was convinced that every person in that valley was going to be waiting for them. They would have the advantage of picking the time and place to start the battle. And the element of surprise? Forget about it.

And as Karl von Clausewitz once said (to paraphrase): Without surprise, you're fucked.

As they weaved through the dense network of packed streets into Kandahar proper, the radio chatter started up among the convoy, pleading for this car or that car to slow down.

Red looked at Ringo, who like himself, couldn't help laughing at the absurdity of it all. They could not have created a bigger signature for the enemy to target if they tried. Red glanced along the houses and buildings. He grew more and more nervous as dark, shadowy figures moved and leaped from rooftop to rooftop. The setting was perfect for an ambush.

Barely a few days earlier, a special forces team had suffered two casualties from a grenade attack. Red turned his attention back to the muddled panorama of overloaded trucks, dust, donkeys, carts, and Toyotas, horns blaring as chaos flowed through Kandahar. Standing in the middle of one intersection was an Afghan traffic cop waving his hands in the motions of directing traffic, but there was no relationship between the direction of traffic and his hand gestures. The convoy ignored the cop and decided to move their own way. In order to push through the madness, they jockeyed through every opening they could find, even if it meant taking the sidewalk.

Thirty minutes later, the drive through Kandahar was over. Thank God and praise Allah—no "Black Hawk Down" that day.

The convoy turned off of Route 1 and moved toward the north. They drove by Firebase Gecko, formerly Mullah Omar's fortress headquarters and now occupied by U.S. forces. A team from the 19th Special Forces Group was getting ready to collect their crew of Afghan fighters, put them in helicopters, and meet them at the objective in two days.

Just to the east of Gecko was a steep wall of hills. Their road stretched through a pass in the hills and down to the Rûd-e Arghandāb (Arghandāb River) valley. The Rûd-e Arghandāb ran north-south through western Kandahar, providing water for the extensive orchards for which the region was once famous. The Rûd-e Arghandāb fed the Arghandāb Band (Arghandāb Lake) formed by a dam built by American engineers in the 1960s when the United States had extensive overseas assistance programs.

Thanks in part to USAID and in part to Pashtun hard work and ingenuity, local warlords lost their grip on the region, and the Arghandāb became one of the most verdant and prosperous places in Afghanistan.

Red was familiar with this place, because he once called it home.

• • •

Red's father had worked for USAID as an agriculture research scientist. His mother had been a secretary with the Department of State. They lived in Afghanistan from 1966 to 1970, in a nice little house in Kabul. He and his brother attended the American International School of Kabul, where they learned the local language. Later, they lived in Islamabad, Pakistan, for almost five years.

Red was proud of his father's achievements in turning huge swaths of the country into verdant fields, and he was proud that Americans could, at least in those days, be thought of as friends of the Afghan people.

When the Taliban and al Qaeda took over Afghanistan and declared war on America, many in this region remembered his father and the other Americans who had once helped them build this country. The hearts and minds of the citizens were on their side, not al Qaeda's. Red would soon have the occasion to tap this sympathy, especially among middle-class middle-aged men whose sons became their guides and interpreters.

A severe drought, combined with the disastrous consequences of the Soviet invasion, had long since dried up the river as far south as Kandahar. During the Soviet-Afghan war, the Russians were repeatedly attacked from these orchards, called "green zones," which were a favorite place for freedom fighters to run into after ambushing the enemy. The Soviets in turn defoliated vast sections of the green zones, and the once-fertile Rûd-e Arghandāb was turned into this bleak battlefield, this open sore.

Decades from now, maybe, the Rûd-e Arghandāb would return to its lush, prewar state. But for now, the landscape was bleak and utterly devoid of any living thing, a vast expanse of stunted orchards and all-pervasive sands and cemeteries that reminds one of the futility of human endeavor.

• • •

The convoy followed the dried canal north into a cratered wasteland, where even a scorpion could no longer find sustenance. The paved road ended at the top of a pass, and the valley opened up under them as they drove down the other side of the hill. A thin, fragile stretch of green followed the river, contrasting sharply with the rest of the landscape.

They had no sooner crossed the canal and turned north up the canal road when convoy commander Major R. called for a piss stop. They had been on the road for only an hour. The temperature was climbing to over 120 degrees, and the dust muddied their sweat and blinded their eyes. They moved forward another 500 meters and rolled to a stop.

Red got on the radio and called that they had stopped. Traditional mud and adobe compounds were on both sides of the road. He got out of the car with Ringo and Doc Ken, stretched his legs, and watched a pack of local tribesmen staring back at him. Every time they stopped they attracted a crowd. Like in his father's black and white photographs of 1960s Afghanistan, it was almost always young men and boys, and some young girls, who would come out and surround them. Girls over 12 were considered women and were confined to their homes. A few older men would join the group; they weren't afraid of the Americans and would crowd around them to the point that they had to order them to step back.

Rock stayed on the machine gun. Diligence was critical, and it was unsafe to get too comfortable; after all, there were bound to be Taliban sympathizers in their midst, among the crowd. Think of these people as your pals and you were bound to get a cap popped into your ass or a frag thrown into your ride. For the most part, they told anyone who approached—in no uncertain terms and regardless of their intentions—to move on. Fuck the mister nice guy charade.

Flipper was the exception. There he was, a few cars back, being his friendly self with the locals. His other nickname was

"Smilin' Joe" because he always had the same shit-eating grin on his face. Red watched him get out of his GMV and mash with the kids. A crowd started to form. He just stood in the center, smiling and laughing. Red was eager to remind him that they were there to hunt terrorists, not bond with the locals. Flipper was taking the idea of "winning the hearts and minds" a little too far—far enough to get them killed. Plus it was getting late, and they had other concerns.

• • •

And chief among them was Oreo cookies. They were in the middle of a barren wasteland, and they had honest-to-God, real-life, contents-written-in-English-on-the-side-of-the-package, true-blue American Oreo "Double Stuf" cookies. They savored them as a culinary delight like no other. Captain Alan, being a fan of both cookies and chocolate, had talked a teammate out of a three-pack that his wife had sent as a care package. With ceremony befitting the gravity of the situation, he carefully twisted and separated the upper cookie shell from the rich creamy center.

It had been months since the men of Beast 85 could even think about such a delicious and decadent feast as an Oreo cookie. Five long months, during which they had been all over Afghanistan—from the city of Kandahar to the central areas of Kabul and Bagram, and as far south as the Pakistani border near Spin Buldak, west toward Laskar Gah and Geresk, east to the Zabul province, and all along the wide-flowing Helmand River.

Every inch of their journey was marked by hours driven through the inhospitable, tortured earth of Afghanistan. Temperatures consistently topped 120 degrees, and naturally occurring ground water was rare. In every direction they turned, there was lunarscape. Apparently the elements had conspired to remove this warring land, dispersing it particle by particle. The sun baked the countryside into a fine powder, the wind lifted it, and the land danced away, interrupted only by the unlikely rain shower that sent it earthward again in muddy droplets.

Accordingly, their diet consisted of whatever hermetically sealed packaging could withstand the constant assault of wind, heat, and dust. Military rations, generously named "meals ready to eat," or MREs, made up the bulk of their daily calories. Sure, these were "meals" in the sense that they were food. But what precisely they were "ready" for, or whether they were edible at all, was debatable. Nonetheless, they contained calories and gut-filling mass that they could turn to at least once a day for sustenance. The remainder of their daily intake consisted of drained tuna packets and protein bars. Oh, yeah—and bottled water.

While the terrain of Afghanistan is rocky and dry, it is not without its wells, irrigation-fed green zones or whatever remains of them after the Soviet occupation, and industrious roadside water peddlers that service the cross-country truckers and cabbies.

Maybe you believe that a special forces soldier quenches his thirst from little more than roadside cacti and solar stills in the dust. This represents an overactive imagination fueled by pop culture. Recall the line from Barry Sadler's *Ballad of the Green Beret*: "Trained to live off nature's land; trained in combat, hand to hand."

While it is true that Beast 85 could have gotten its water from local sources, treated it with gallons of artery-clogging chlorine and pounds of headache-inducing iodine tablets, to do so would have quickly ended any further exploration of Afghanistan.

But the captain knew (and Red especially knew, having spent much of his childhood in Afghanistan), "If you drink the water, you die." To elaborate, if you ingest anything that has come in contact with the local water, you will wish you were dead.

Imagine your daily activities—from brushing your teeth to washing the dishes or an apple or your body. Now imagine that every drop, every molecule of water that squeaks past your lips and enters your system has the potential to send your guts into churning fury, an uncontrollable explosiveness that induces instantaneous panic whenever you realize you are more than a frantic 6-second waddle from the commode.

Locals don't seem to mind drinking the water, regardless of the source. The captain remembered watching in stunned awe as a Pashtun tribesman scooped water with his bare hands from a muddy irrigation ditch along the road and drank it. Farther upstream, he saw others enjoying the rivulet: a man rinsing his turban and another man giving himself a bath. Still farther upstream, a donkey sauntered across and stopped briefly to enjoy the cool respite and take a drink. For the locals, in addition to washing clothes and drinking, it is imperative they wash their feet five times a day before they pray.

Every drop of Beast 85's water had to be accounted for. For planning purposes, this meant four gallons per man per day. Doing the math, their team of 12 operators and one interpreter had to carry 52 gallons of water for every day of an operation. That's 11 5-gallon water jugs or five cases of bottled water. For a typical 14-day patrol, 728 gallons of water would be consumed. Typically they would carry a five-day supply, and additional water would be air-dropped to them at preplanned locations.

The team carried a combination of 5-gallon jugs and cases of bottles. The containers would be piled, stacked, and strapped to every inch of the vehicles. Initially the load would be oppressive. But as the days went on, the containers would empty, legroom would expand, and their parched throats would be refreshed.

"Refreshed" had its own meaning in Afghanistan. Imagine being hot, dry, and thirsty and really parched, with only super-heated water to quench your thirst, having to weigh whether it's worth the risk of scalding your mouth. Every bottle of water that rode along the dusty trail with Beast 85 would hit 110 degrees, even in the relative shade of the vehicles.

Between the hot water and the bland food, you can understand the captain's hankering for that Oreo cookie. Then, in an instant, unfulfilled pleasure turned to utter dismay as the cookie tumbled out of his hand, rolled along its edge, and came to rest on the ground, stuffed side up. Murphy's Law states (as soldiers are well aware), "Drop a peanut butter–covered cracker and it will invariably land sticky side down." But there was the captain's Oreo, lying face up on the ground, his reward for months of MREs and hot water. He counted backward from five, invoking the rule from childhood, as he bent to pick it up.

As his fingers closed on the cookie, it all came rushing back—the sewer water mixed with drinking water, tainted with unpronounceable strains of who-knows-what, the days of misery and sickness that would follow if it entered your system. This realization was like a vacuum, sucking the joy out of the moment.

In an instant, the captain's reward had been transformed into a germ-infested Trojan horse appealing on the outside, yet packed with peril for anyone foolish enough to actually ingest it. He let go and left the cookie to be covered in dust. In Afghanistan, there was no such thing as a 5-second rule.

· · ·

So the word went out to roll. The road was wide and well traveled but very rutted and bumpy. It followed the canal on the right and the green zone on the left. Red was more and more convinced that word of their approach traveled well ahead of them. There was only one road north, and they were on it. The convoy of men were like trout in a barrel.

Thankfully, the plugger was now up and running. Red checked the map, radioed that they were moving, and listened to Ringo bitch about their mission, the heat, about being in Afghanistan, and anything else he could think of. Things were proceeding like normal, if normal is being in a sitting-duck convoy waiting for an inevitable ambush.

They had traveled no more than half a kilometer when the word came over the satellite communications (SATCOM) radio that the original SEAL mission had slid off the plate and now they wanted to play, wanted a part in the operation. The problem was that they were just leaving Kandahar Airfield and wanted the convoy to wait for them. Major R. agreed to wait, so they stopped again and waited for the SEAL platoon to catch up. Ringo, who had been in the marines as a recon guy, was given the perfect catalyst to rage over the Navy SEALs.

Red enjoyed the diatribe. It was fun to listen to a true maestro of angst at full bubble. The heat continued to rise; they were drawing a larger and larger crowd of curious Afghans, and their timeline was being pushed back minute by minute. They waited and waited, and watched their sectors for the Taliban gunman they were sure would take a shot at them.

An hour later, still no contact from the navy. Just as Major R. was getting ready to push forward without them, they showed up. Finally, the convoy could start to roll north again.

The time was 1400 hours, and they had not moved nearly far enough. The radio reminded them that they needed to try to make up for lost time. So now the major was in a rush. Red passed the word to Ringo that they needed to pick it up. Rock in the back on the M240B was going to get punished. Red planned to have Doc Ken relieve Rock at the next stop. Being in the front gave them the advantage of not eating dust or having to accordion by speeding up and slowing down, which is something a 30-vehicle convoy always has to deal with.

The road north followed the Rûd-e Arghandāb. The dry canal, with few small towns on the far bank, was on the right, and walled orchards were on the left. This continued for about 20 kilometers, until the road crossed the canal and the Rûd-e Arghandāb as it turned east and they continued north.

The easy part was over. The route was never as clear from that point forward. The road crossed the Rûd-e Arghandāb once more at a town called Sayd Alim Kaliav. There was an Afghan army checkpoint at the far end of the bridge, and a soldier waved them down rather than through. Red asked Ringo to slow down. The soldier wanted *baksheesh*, or a bribe, to allow them to pass. Rock pointed his machine gun in the soldier's general direction as Red told the guy in English (a language Red was sure the soldier did not understand) to go fuck himself (the intent of which he was sure to understand). The soldier's expression hardened for a second, but he knew it was a fight he could not win. He muttered a few insults in Pashtun under his breath as they moved past him through the town, toward the first set of hills they were going to cross.

The Afghan army was really a group of armed thugs that worked for the local warlord. This soldier was a little more brazen than most Red had seen. Usually they recognized that the Americans were stronger and respected them for that. Red would have stopped and confronted the guy for that kind of threatening gesture any other time, but they were in a hurry. He knew as they moved through these checkpoints, the details of their position, strength, and direction were being reported to Afghans on both sides of the conflict. There was no way they were going to approach in stealth, as the Operations Order claimed they would, but Red had known that for more than a week.

The map and its relative waypoints started to lose continuity. The road would fade away and then pick back up in the dust. They would move forward, and the next waypoint on the GPR would start to drift to the left or right until they passed it a few hundred meters broadside rather than moving from one to the other.

The terrain started to become hilly with lots of dry rocky wadis, but the course was north. There was only one donkey trail going that way, and they were on it. The land was broken, hilly, and depopulated for the next 30 kilometers. The countryside north of Kandahar was a vast expanse of rocks and cemeteries, cratered donkey trails, and ruined compound walls that had long spread into the Pashtun soul, their children stunted by dust and defoliants, their eyes seemingly oblivious to the presence of yet another caravan of invaders.

Red began to feel the stress of pushing forward into the unknown using imprecise maps, with waypoints taken from those maps, and a plugger that confirmed that things were not as they appeared on the map.

Rock was now resting in the crew cab, and Doc Ken was in the back at the machine gun. They pushed through the scabrous hills out onto a large wide plain with a range of mountains behind them stretching from west to east. The plain was absolutely barren. Red dubbed the place the "Bad Lands." The road turned onto the plains, and they stopped for another piss break. They couldn't see anything green around them. They were lost in the midst of ethereal emptiness.

It was 1630 hours, and the sun was sinking in the sky. They still had a long way to go. Red's multiband interteam radio, which was capable of great things, decided that it wasn't going to pick up any signals from the major. This was a positive thing. He had been jamming the airways with commands and directions to move faster, to do this and that, but they couldn't hear any of it anyway. Major R. was freaking out, but it was his plan to stress about, not Red's.

They found themselves on a terrain of absolute desolation and strange natural phenomena at every turn—the carcass of an abandoned Soviet tank; a clear-air tornado pulling dust thousands of feet into the air on its silent path across the plains; the heat furnace of an inescapable sun—anyone stranded out in this country would be dead in less than a day. Other than the occasional cargo truck rolling by, there was no indication of the presence of living man.

It was nature at its deadliest, in the same land that had swallowed Alexander the Great and countless more would-be invaders. Beast 85's trip across these badlands would be truly biblical.

# CHAPTER 2

# THE MAKING OF A GREEN BERET

*A beret is perhaps the most useless of hats. It doesn't block rain well, nor does it shade the eyes, nor is it particularly warm in cold weather. Yet numerous books have been written about the Green Beret, movies made, and songs written. People have died trying to earn the right to wear one. And many more have died after earning that right.*

*For all their lore, Green Berets are not Rambos with a machine gun in one hand, a grenade in the other, and a knife clenched between the teeth. They are the quiet professionals.*

*The core of special forces is the individual soldier. These individuals are drawn together into the basic operating unit of special forces: the A-team. An A-team such as Beast 85 is a highly trained, cohesive force that is capable of a multitude of divergent tasks, operating either independently or in concert with strategic-level forces at any location around the world. During the Vietnam War, special forces soldiers were awarded a higher percentage of decorations than any unit before or since.*

*You've probably heard the terms in the news: Green Beret; A-team; Special Operations Force; Delta Force; SEAL; Nightstalker. You may have seen John Wayne and Sylvester Stallone portraying Green Berets in movies. You may even have read Robin Moore's classic book about special forces operations in Vietnam, or more recently seen or read* Black Hawk Down, *yet few people outside the closed circle of special operations know exactly what special forces do or how the men who wear the green beret are selected, trained, and operate. The men of Beast 85 were reservists with full-time civilian status and a unique perspective from being torn from their ordinary lives, put on active duty, and sent off to fight on the frontlines of the war against terrorism.*

R ed is a 38-year-old information technology (IT) professional working in northern Virginia. He has a wife, two children, and a house in the suburbs. He has lived a normal middle-class life except for one detail. When he was 18, he joined the army and started volunteering for everything he could. When he left the active army four years later in 1988, he was a Green Beret, a member of the U.S. Army Special Forces.

Red was born in 1964 in New Haven, Connecticut. His dad was finishing his Ph.D. in agronomy at the University of Rhode Island. When he was six months old, his family moved to Indonesia, to a small rubber plantation on the island of Sumatra, which his dad managed for the Firestone Rubber Company. It was 1965, the year of living dangerously, the year of civil war between the Malay and the Chinese. In the midst of these massacres, his family was forced to flee the war and return to the States.

By 1966, they were living in Kabul, Afghanistan, where his dad worked with USAID as an agricultural research scientist. He was two, his brother "Evan" was four, and they lived on the quiet side of a quiet city on the edge of the civilized world. No television, no satellites, no long-distance phones. They had a nice house with apricot trees in the back. He remembered it being very green. He attended the American International School in Kabul for first grade and half of second grade.

His family then moved to Turkey, where he attended the Department of Defense School at Balgat Air Force Base outside Ankara. Red loved Turkey. Great food, lots of trips to the coast. His parents were young and had lots of American and Turkish friends. The family stayed in Ankara until 1974 when the war with Greece started. Red remembers antiaircraft batteries being set up outside of their apartment. His dad was transferred again, and they went to Saigon, Vietnam.

Vietnam was a strange place. Henry Kissinger wanted USAID to bring American families to Saigon to show the world that the war was over. Red saw a C-5 airplane full of orphans crash right into a suburb of Saigon. Then he witnessed a napalm strike on a village on the other side of the Saigon River, and he was evacuated with his mom in April 1975. His brother was at a boarding school in the Philippines. His dad would stay in Saigon until the very end, among the last people to be evacuated to Subic Bay, Philippines, aboard a U.S. Air Force jet. The rest of the family feared that he would remain trapped in Vietnam, but he escaped, and the family reunited in Florida.

Between 1975 and 1977 they lived in a cool, leafy, peaceful town in northern Virginia where life was great, but employment prospects were slim. Red's dad signed up for another tour of duty with USAID, this time to Islamabad, Pakistan.

During their stay in Islamabad, the Mullahs took over Persia, and the Soviets invaded Afghanistan. On 21 November 1979, a crowd of radical Islamic "students" stormed the U.S. Embassy in Islamabad, burning it down along with the entire American compound, killing two Americans, one of whom was a U.S. Marine Corps (USMC) embassy guard Red knew. This was a reprisal over the failed U.S. attempt to free American hostages in Tehran. The mob then gave chase to the children who were attending the International School.

Red remembers being chased by a gang of Pakistani university students through empty classrooms and corridors. He ran and ran as they gave chase, then tumbled, collected himself, and just kept running. He tumbled again and broke his arm.

The next day, he and his family were evacuated to the States. They stayed in northern Virginia for a couple of months before being sent to the Philippines. On 21 August 1983, former Senator Benigno "Ninoy" Aquino was murdered on the tarmac of Manila International Airport the moment he stepped on Philippine soil. Aquino had come home from exile in the United States to persuade President Marcos to restore freedom and democracy. He sacrificed his life for the cause.

Three weeks after Aquino's murder, Red moved back to the States to start his adult life. Traveling had taught him a couple of things. He had seen with his own eyes all kinds of violence, war, and fundamentalism. He had seen the power of goodwill and courage, too—the goodwill and courage of people like his father and mother.

Red eventually joined the U.S. Army. A year and a half later he was the junior 91BSP (special forces medic) on ODA 524, B Company, 1st Battalion, 5th SFGA (Special Forces Group [Airborne]). Later they made him an 18D, the new term for special forces medic. He stayed in the 5th group for a few years and was deployed three quarters of the time around the United States and in the Middle East. Then he opted out of active duty.

To keep Red and others who left active duty in the reserve system, the army enticed them with tuition reimbursement for college and a stipend for attending monthly drills. During Red's undergraduate and graduate studies, he stayed in the National Guard because it was a source of money and a fun summer job. He went to Central America five times, and attended free-fall school, sniper school, and the advanced urban combat course.

He then went to George Mason University in northern Virginia. He stayed in the National Guard and mobilized with Desert Storm in 1991 just as he graduated from college. Desert Storm was uneventful for Red; he sat around in the desert for three months and then went home.

When the war was over, he was out of school and out of the army. He joined the Department of State for three years, working at several embassies in Latin America and the Far East. His chief motivation to stay in the National Guard, he'll admit, was to pick up the small retirement check that was offered after 20 years. He got married, had two children, worked for a couple of civilian outfits as an IT expert and then, about two years ago, he was selected for the rank of master sergeant and was given a special forces A-team as the noncommissioned officer in charge.

Anyone who has served in uniform has heard the comment: "Things will be done differently in wartime." The idea is that somehow everyone will step it up a notch or two when the bullets start flying. Beast 85 was about to learn that the reality is quite the opposite.

. . .

Prior to 9/11, Bravo Company, 3rd Battalion, 20th Special Forces Group (in which Red is operations sergeant of Special Forces Operational Detachment Alpha 2085) met monthly at Fort A. P. Hill in Virginia for drill. Drill weekends usually were from Friday evening through Sunday afternoon. They would jump out of airplanes, blow up stuff at the range, practice patrolling, and check the administrative blocks they needed to stay current and up to speed. The currency requirements were pushed down to them by the U.S. Army's Special Operations Command.

They served two masters as members of the Virginia Army National Guard. First, they served their chain of command: 3rd Battalion of 20th SFGA, headquartered in Florida; then 20th Special Forces Group, headquartered in Alabama; then the active-duty U.S. Army Special Operations Command (USASOC) at Fort Bragg, North Carolina. Second, they served the state of Virginia, through the 91st Troop Command, an administrative unit.

Their relationship with the special forces community was pretty straightforward: training requirements, annual training missions, and extra money was allocated to special forces from USASOC.

Their relationship with the state of Virginia was more administrative, providing them with a place to meet and drill, paying them, taking care of their personal records, pay records, providing travel vouchers, and answering requests for orders. The state of Virginia inherited their company from the 11th Special Forces Group, which was part of the army reserve, not the National Guard, and was RIF'd (reduction in forces), or chopped, after the Gulf War in 1992. The 11th Special Forces Group was deactivated, but their company at Fort A. P. Hill was simply added to the National Guard's 20th Special Forces Group. So they became members of the Virginia National Guard.

The Virginia Army National Guard thought it was cool to have a special forces company for about six months until it buckled under the disproportionately huge administrative burden they added to the state. Their company put in more requests for army schools, more requests for orders, for overseas travel, for more of everything than any other unit in the state. They also received all kinds of specialty pay, went overseas for annual training, and attended one or two schools per man per year, all of which the National Guard was unaccustomed to.

The Virginia Army National Guard is not something Red considered cutting edge in its management practices. They were a hugely bureaucratic good-ol'-boy outfit. Red's company very quickly came to blows with the 91st Troop Command and the state headquarters unit over a number of pay problems due to late or lost paperwork. Although they continued to chug along and do what they needed to do to remain proficient, they were always in a battle with the state over something. Pay problems that just wouldn't go away resulted in inspector general investigations and congressional complaints.

# CHAPTER 3

# 9/11

R ed's team was at the special forces advanced urban combat
course in Anniston, Alabama, on 11 September 2001. Entire
teams participate in the three-week course to learn advanced
combat skills in built-up areas—the closest analogy is SWAT
tactics, except the urban combat course is far more violent. The
fourth day into the course was 11 September 2001. Red remembers the day well. His team, like the four other teams attending
the course, had rented large vans to transport men and gear
between the ranges and the barracks. As they drove up to the
range, one of the instructors approached the van and told them
that an airplane had just hit one of the towers of the World Trade
Center (WTC). Red assumed it was an accident. He turned on the
radio and tuned to an AM station that was broadcasting CBS
News from New York. One of the towers was burning, people
were jumping for their lives, and there was lots of speculation
about what had happened. As the news announcer continued, a
second plane hit the other tower. When the second plane hit,
someone from another van who was also listening to the radio
yelled that another plane had hit. All training came to a halt.

They knew then that it was a terrorist attack. Red called
home and told his wife that the United States was under attack,
to go to the school, get their daughter out of class, go home, and

watch TV for any emergency instructions. His wife had not had the TV on that morning, so this came as quite a shock to her. She must have heard something in the tone of his voice, and did exactly what he asked her to do without questioning him. The team continued to train for the rest of the day, as the news on the radio became more and more grim.

That night, they drove to the local Wal-Mart to watch the news on television. It was the first time any of them had seen the WTC fall. The planes looked like a magician's trick as they simply disappeared into the sides of the towers, with nothing happening for the briefest of moments. The planes just disappeared. Then the towers had to release the energy they absorbed and surrender to their awful fate of complete and total destruction. Red could not believe what he was watching.

• • •

Each generation is defined by major historical events. The captain was born too late for the 1960s and 1970s sex parties, and was still too young to partake in the greedy excesses of the 1980s. In the 1990s, with the raging bull stock market, the advent of the Internet, and the kids of Generation-Y who mastered Web surfing by the age of three, his generation's coming of age was an afterthought. There were exceptions, though: 20-something "dot-com" millionaires and wealthy investment banking wunderkinds made headlines. But for the most part, they were known mainly as the union of the aforementioned hot-blooded generations, labeled by at least one popular magazine as "The Lost Generation."

The captain's indelible memories of the day the Twin Towers were felled and the Pentagon breached were accompanied by an overwhelming sense of lost innocence about the tragic arrival of international terrorism on home soil. Coincidentally, Captain Alan was honing the very tools he would use to fight just such a foe.

Within a few days, the focus of the United States was turned toward Afghanistan, the Taliban, al Qaeda, and a man named Osama bin Laden. Prior to that fateful day, most Americans were unaware of the thread that connected these four elements. Even now, many Americans simply cannot comprehend the rationale behind the attacks.

Bin Laden has been reported to be Saudi Arabian, but his ancestral home was in Hadramawt in southern Yemen. While his father was a Yemeni, bin Laden's mother was a Saudi. Bin Laden's father moved to Saudi Arabia in 1930 to found the bin Laden Group, a construction company, with his brothers. The company garnered numerous Saudi government contracts and built everything from mosques in Mecca and Medina to highways and palaces. The bin Laden family eventually amassed a fortune estimated at several billion dollars.

Osama bin Laden was born in 1957 in Saudi Arabia, the 17th son of 51 children, and was raised under strict Islamic rules. His father died when he was 13. He attended King Adul-Aziz University in Jeddah, Saudi Arabia, and while he was there, the Soviets invaded Afghanistan. Bin Laden traveled to Afghanistan and Pakistan as part of the mujaheedeen (Holy Warrior) resistance movement. In 1984, he built a way station in Peshawar, Pakistan, where new recruits would stop on their way to fight in Afghanistan. By 1986, he had six camps training recruits. He fought in several battles against the Soviets, including the battle of Jalalabad. The mujaheedeen was receiving support from the CIA against the Soviets; thus, bin Laden was an ally of the United States at this time.

In 1988, bin Laden decided to separate his group from the mujaheedeen, and he called his group al Qaeda, *the base*. When the Soviets withdrew from Afghanistan in 1989, bin Laden returned to Saudi Arabia, and al Qaeda set up its headquarters in Peshawar, Pakistan, from 1989 to 1991.

In Saudi Arabia, bin Laden began making public speeches denouncing the Saudi government. They placed a travel ban on him. When his countrymen took part in Operation Desert Storm, bin Laden became incensed: in his view, the Saudis had sold their souls to the Christian crusaders. Bin Laden was forced to leave the country and go to Pakistan, then on to Afghanistan where he tried to broker an alliance between several muja-heedeen factions. There were at least two attempts on his life, forcing him to leave the country for Sudan in late 1991.

The strict Islamic ideology of Sudan's National Islamic Front attracted him. Additionally, this pariah regime needed his money and construction expertise. While continuing to foster his al Qaeda group, bin Laden worked on various Sudanese govern-ment–sponsored projects throughout the country.

Bin Laden set up his headquarters in Khartoum. The Saudi intelligence agency made several botched attempts on his life in this time period, and the Sudanese government froze his assets in 1993. With international pressure increasing, the Sudanese government asked bin Laden to leave in 1996. He went to the only place he could: Afghanistan.

Once ensconced there, he announced a jihad against the United States, calling for all Muslims to "kill Americans and their allies, civilian and military." He set up several training camps for terrorists and sent agents abroad. Al Qaeda was behind the Khobar Towers bombing that killed 19 Americans in Riyadh in

1996, and the bombings of American embassies in Kenya and Tanzania in 1998.

Meanwhile in Afghanistan, a Wahhabist movement known as the Taliban and financed by Saudi Arabia, U.S. oil giant Unocal, and Pakistan had swept the Northern Alliance from power, pinning Commander Massoud to less than 5 percent of the country in the northeast. Wahhabism is an austere, puritanical form of Islam that insists on a literal interpretation of the Koran. Extreme Wahhabists harbor a dangerous superiority complex. Since their faith represents God's third and most recent manifestation of his will to mankind, God's old teachings of Judaism and Christianity must absolutely be denounced and replaced by his true will. Infidels, referred to as "the worst of Allah's creatures," must be converted or killed because "Allah hates them."

Wahhabists divide the world in two: the House of Islam, *Dar al-Islam*, where Koranic Law is upheld, and the House of War, *Dar al-Harb*, which is peopled by infidels who, in due time, will surrender to the caliphate. There shall be no peace until Islam triumphs and the world is united under the caliphate.

The internationalization of Wahhabism began with the first oil shock in 1973, when Saudi Arabia, suddenly flush with money, began financing Wahhabi schools, known as madrassas, throughout the world. Seeking to defeat the Communist influence in the Middle East, the United States allied itself with Saudi Arabia. This strange bedfellows' alliance allowed Wahhabism to spread like wildfire. Depite its absence from Afghanistan until the late 1970s, over a period of less than two decades, Wahhabism became a dominant faith among antigovernment activists in nearly all Muslim countries. Wahhabism stretched from Indonesia to Morocco, and its jihad soon engulfed Algeria, parts of Indonesia, and many other Islamic regions. It claimed hundreds of thousands of lives in the process. Yet Saudi support for fundamentalist madrassas kept growing, and the U.S. government failed to address the threat until 9/11 claimed 3,000 lives on American soil. Remember two figures: all 19 hijackers were Wahhabis; 15 of them were Saudis.

The worst of Allah's creatures Westerners may well be, but in the eyes of a Wahhabi, the strategic priority is to get rid of other Muslims first, such as the tolerant, enlightened Sufis, the Shi'as, and the mainstream Sunnis. Extreme Wahhabism views all these faiths genocidally. The Taliban's first campaigns of mass murder were targeted at the Shi'as of central Afghanistan. Thousands were killed in a brutal campaign against the Hazaras, a peaceful nation that had embraced Shi'a Islam. In 1997, 10,000 Hazara men, women, and children were summarily executed in the city of Mazar-i-Sharif in northern Afghanistan. Throughout Afghanistan, processions were attacked with knives, guns, and grenades; dozens of Hazara towns and villages were razed in a brutal campaign of ethnic cleansing that lasted between 1997 and 2001.

By March 2001, Mullah Omar had decreed that two colossal statues of the Buddha, carved into the sandstone cliffs of Bamiyan in the Hazara province of central Afghanistan, represented an insult to Islam (the Hazaras converted from Buddhism to Islam in the fourteenth century, yet kept the idols). Omar rejected a Saudi proposal to have a concrete wall built in front of the two statues. On 12 March, he destroyed them in a fury of tank, mortar, dynamite, antiaircraft, and rocket fire. Then the Wahhabite turned his ire against the local people, who were, in his eyes, "guilty of keeping idolatrous images of humans and animals" and who "repeatedly violated the Islamic prohibition against sacred images." Food supplies were burned; upwards of 40,000 Hazaras were starved to death or murdered. As Beast 85 would soon discover, the Hazaras would supply many a committed CIA informant and anti-Taliban fighter.

In the meantime, devout Wahhabite bin Laden had become an instrumental purveyor of men, weapons, and money to the Taliban regime. On the eve of 9/11, al Qaeda men posing as reporters carried out the assassination of Mullah Omar's and bin Laden's archenemy, Afghan resistance leader Ahmed Shah Massoud. By then it was clear that the Taliban had become blood brothers with al Qaeda. Shortly after 9/11, President George W. Bush issued an ultimatum to the Taliban, demanding, among other things:

*That they deliver bin Laden and other al Qaeda leaders in Afghanistan to the United States.*

*That they release all imprisoned foreign nationals.*

*That they protect journalists, diplomats, and aid workers in the country.*

*That they close terrorist training camps and turn over all terrorists.*

*That they give the United States free access to those camps to ensure that they were closed.*

None of these demands were met. The Taliban refused to even communicate with the United States. They issued communiqués through their embassy in Pakistan. They demanded, in turn, that the United States prove that it was bin Laden behind the 9/11 attacks. The United States then went to the United Nations (UN). On 18 September 2001, the UN Security Council issued a resolution demanding that the Taliban turn over bin Laden and shut down his terrorist training camps.

While these demands were being traded back and forth, the U.S. military began planning what was initially called Operation Infinite Justice. It was felt that the name's religious connotations were too inflammatory, so its name was changed to Operation Enduring Freedom.

By 7 October, American and British special forces were on the ground conducting reconnaissance missions and making contact with the Northern Alliance. The war officially began at 1630 GMT on that day with air strikes against numerous targets throughout Afghanistan. By 13 November, the Taliban was in massive retreat all across Afghanistan.

• • •

Red and his team remained in urban combat training for the next two-and-a-half weeks, finishing it up in early October. By the time they finished, the word was being spread that the National Guard special forces were going to mobilize. A few people were called up, but none of the line companies or teams.

Red returned to his home and a brand-new job, which he started 5 October 2001. What was going on in Afghanistan filled the news. The United States had given the Taliban an ultimatum, which Red suspected they would ignore. He was right.

So away they went. Elements of 5th Special Forces Group, which are geographically aligned with the Middle East and central Asia, rolled in to support the Northern Alliance. Red was familiar with their missions: Hook up with the elements that are resisting their common enemy, and help them out. It was a classic unconventional warfare mission, something that special forces had been training to do since Vietnam.

• • •

The drill on 17 November was at Fort A. P. Hill. The company was told in no uncertain terms that there was a chance they would be called up for Operation Enduring Freedom. There was going to be a mobilization of the National Guards' special forces, but who, and when, was still being hashed out.

By mid-November it was clear that the decision had been made that Bravo Company, 3rd Battalion (B/3/20th), was on the short list for mobilization, along with one other company from each of the line companies, and a battalion headquarters element. They were going to mobilize a battalion, but rather than take the entire battalion, they allowed one company from each battalion to be called up.

This served to allow each of the battalions to send their best company to the war. The 19th Special Forces Group was doing the exact same thing. Although they had just finished their annual training, they were told that the plan was to activate the company very close to the first of the year. The activation would be for one to two years under Title 10 of the U.S. Code. In other words, B/3/20th was going to war.

Later on, Red learned that the original war plans called for a 40 percent casualty rate with the first group of special forces sent into Afghanistan. The estimate climbed as high as 50 percent for when the war pushed south of the capital, Kabul, to the southern Pashtun areas of the country. In other words, Pentagon planners thought there was a 50 percent chance that people like those in Beast 85 would die in combat.

In addition to the battalion from the 20th and the 19th Special Forces Groups, everyone in special forces on inactive reserve status or individual mobilization status was called up for a two-year tour. Two years is a lot of time for a reserve guy.

"How is Afghanistan?" Red remembered one reserve guy asking during the briefing.

"Hot, dry, and mountainous in the south, and very mountainous and cold in the north."

Red dropped $2,000 on knives, canteens, and mountain gear, and informed his employer that he was being called up to active duty the next Monday. He had only been working there a little more than a month. He recommended they consult with corporate counsel about what the law allowed during his deployment. His employer was surprised they didn't even have to pay him. But thankfully, they made up the difference between his paycheck and army pay, which took a huge burden off of his chest. At least money wasn't going to be the problem.

• • •

November went by in a flash. Red spent as much time as possible with his family. He and his wife wrote their wills. He gave her power of attorney over everything. His daughter was five at the time, his son just two. "Dad is going overseas to do something for our country." "Why can't he do it at home?" "No, honey, this is something Dad can't do from home." The kids couldn't understand.

Over Thanksgiving, e-mail correspondence was flying around with ideas on where he and his team might be deployed. Word came back that they were going to storm some al Qaeda training camp in western Somalia. Yet other messages insisted they were flying into eastern Ethiopia, northern Erithrea, or even southern Sudan.

• • •

Within a few weeks of completing the urban combat course, each member of the team experienced a scene similar to this:

First, he would have received notification of his pending deployment. That left almost a month to tie up loose ends, visit family members, and pack up his gear. Then he, his wife, possibly his young children, would stand facing each other on the front porch, with one prevailing thought—one that crosses the mind of every soldier—that he may never again see his family. He might die somewhere in Afghanistan, Pakistan, Ethiopia or Somalia, or God knows where else. His shoulders would have trembled as he took his wife and children in his arms, taking from each other the inspiration, the strength, and the solace before being separated for a grueling 24 months.

Facing this kind of separation from his family taps a wellspring of tearful emotion in a soldier, one he may have never felt before, with an intensity that makes him both giddy and weak.

After a moment that would seem to last an eternity, yet not nearly long enough, he would have kissed his wife and children goodbye, then headed off to mobilize at Fort Bragg, North Carolina.

• • •

And so they converged on their home station: attorneys, teachers, firemen, policemen, carpenters, medics, and electricians. From across the spectrum of civilian professions they came together, transformed from part-time soldiers who trained on weekends and summers to a full-time special forces company, united in their cause and ready to do their duty. What would transpire over the next year would change all of them. Some unit members would return to their lives a year later feeling a deep sense of resentment and dissatisfaction. They would question the very purpose of having reserve component military, and they would separate from their unit as soon as possible upon their return to prevent what they viewed as misuse and abuse in the future.

Other unit members would be indifferent about their experiences and just be happy to move on with the civilian lives they left behind before deployment. But for the men of Beast 85, it would be a year of action and adventure, challenges and achievement. They would be tried and tested time and time again, and throughout each experience, enduring both success and failure, the team would pull together, becoming more and more effective as each personality settled into his role within the group.

Here they were, side by side—the antagonist, the schizophrenic, the dismissive, the disgruntled, the grinning goof, the gun geek, the gorilla, the kleptomaniac, the neophyte, the Cubano, the cranky team sergeant, and the impetuous team leader—ready to take on all enemies. Each of them would have to rely on the others' strengths, put up with the others' annoying idiosyncrasies, expect and plan for the unexpected, and become one unified weapon against terror. Like asylum inmates who, after months of being exposed only to each other, actually begin to think themselves sane, the members of Beast 85 would become increasingly comfortable with the strange conditions of unconventional warfare. Bushy beards and turbans; ballistic body-armor paired with baseball caps; daytime niceties with self-serving local officials followed by nighttime operations conducted against the Taliban tribesmen they protected; the benchmark for "normal" would slide, unceremoniously, toward the unrecognizable.

• • •

They had a two-week plan to go to ranges and shoot and familiarize themselves with all the weapons systems they could get their hands on, shoot mortars, blow up stuff with C-4, go through all of their records, inventory their gear, take a PT test, get a physical, and make sure everyone had his dog tags.

While the additional training was fun and helpful, the administrative checks amounted to insanity. They checked the same things over and over again. The administrative people would note problems, say they were going to fix them, and the next day note the same problem and say they were going to fix it, and the next day note the same problem again and say they were going to fix it. They were the antechamber to hell, and Beast 85 had to pass through their little world before they could take the next step. A week after reporting for duty, some couch colonel at state headquarters went so far as to ask Special Operations Command (SOC) *not* to mobilize Beast 85 because he couldn't comply with the standards to satisfy the federal requirements for activation. While the process was excruciatingly long and unnecessarily unpleasant for the team, they came to realize that they were not going to ship them to the show until well into the following year. To most of them, that was great news. By 22 December 2001 they were back home for the holidays.

Christmas was stressful. Were they going into hell, or were they not? Maybe they'd stay home. The e-mails were cryptic. The invasion of Afghanistan was over, mission accomplished, no need for help, thank you. Horn of Africa was the story of the day. Mogadishu.

Beast 85 was supposed to report for duty on 3 January, but because of a snowstorm that never materialized the date had been postponed until the next day. Red was grateful because he had come down with a high fever that made him unable to report for duty. His wife, too, was elated. She thought he would never have to leave home. Alas, the next day in the early morning he jumped out of bed, mechanically got into the car, and tried to ease the pain in his throat as he silently and steadfastly headed back to Fort A. P. Hill.

They were told that they needed some training in the new radio systems that had not made it down to the Guard but were going to be used in the theater of operations, wherever that may be. In response, they sent Tim, or "T.T. Boy," their communications NCO, to Fort Bragg. They also needed training in calling in close air support (CAS), and they needed to spend some time in mission planning.

They packed up every last thing, cleaned out their team rooms, emptied the supply barn, loaded, inventoried, and got ready to move to Fort Bragg. The state guys wanted them to leave nothing behind, although they were not even sure if they wanted the team to come back to Fort A. P. Hill or not. Red asked the commander of the 91st Troop Command what was going to happen to them when they returned to the Virginia Army National Guard. He replied that they would cross that bridge when they got to it. All full-time National Guard guys that were not going to mobilize with them were reassigned. Bravo Company, 3rd Battalion, 20th Special Forces Group, was pulled off of the Virginia Army National Guard books, reassigned to the federal army under Title 10, and promptly forgotten.

CHAPTER **4**

# FORT BRAGG

*Fort Bragg is where Colonel Aaron Banks and the first ten members of special forces gathered on 19 June 1952 on Smoke Bomb Hill. It is also the home of the 18th Airborne Corps, the 82nd Airborne Division, and* DELTA *Force. The John F. Kennedy Special Warfare Center and School is also located there, where every special forces soldier undergoes assessment and training.*

The madness of rejoining the regular army started almost at once. The army didn't want Beast 85 to report with their personal vehicles. They were going to transport them down to Fort Bragg on tour buses and dump them there. As to who was going to provide transportation for 300 reservists after that—well, that was not the point. The point was that the army didn't want to pay miles on a travel voucher to the guys to drive to Fort Bragg.

Fort Bragg's mobilization unit in-processing center was a collection of support troops that were reservists themselves, but thought they were tough guys. They tried to push Beast 85 around, making threats that they would hold the entire unit if they continued to talk while standing in line, wear their hats in the chow hall, or question any of the stupid decisions they made. They pushed the team through the same silly checks again. Medical check, dental check, finance check, personal records check, again and again. The army's system is not computerized. Things that were identified as wrong get noted again and again without ever being fixed.

An example of the problems with the system is the reserve finance payroll system. The average special forces guy gets two to three extra incentive pays. For instance, in peacetime Red gets his base pay, jump pay for being airborne qualified, foreign language incentive pay for knowing reasonable Spanish, professional pay for being in special forces, and high-altitude, low-opening (HALO) pay. During combat operations there is combat, hardship, and family separation pay, all of which are tax-free. The reserve system can handle two of those, and cannot stop withholding taxes. Unless a willing clerk goes in and cuts another check with the additional pay and the tax refund, Red and others like him don't get their pay.

They stayed at Fort Bragg for almost a month, in open-bay barracks built at the start of World War II. They were in pretty bad shape. Those who were sick on arrival got even sicker. In the twenty-first century, citizen-soldiers from the mightiest nation on earth get to sleep in open barracks in the middle of winter, they get to repeat over and over again the same things to the same stupid clerks, they get sick, and they don't get paid, and they can't feed their families or pay the mortgages on their homes. Meanwhile, they're supposed to win the war on terror.

Yet for some reason the guys kept the faith. Shaped by adversity, their team was getting stronger by the day. Up until this point, they knew that they were going to be reporting to

3rd Special Forces Group—Horn of Africa. Now, 3rd SFGA is geographically aligned to Africa, but had had plenty of experience helping out 5th SFGA in the Central Command, which is in the Middle East. Third SFGA was in Desert Storm *and* in Somalia. Third SFGA had been around for about 13 years since it was reactivated in the 1980s. People wanted out of the 3rd SFGA, which is considered the worst special forces group to be assigned to.

But they were not going to Somalia yet. They were assigned to 1st Battalion, 3rd Special Forces Group, in March and placed on Red Cycle, which meant picking up trash around Fort Bragg, clearing pine cones, manning the funeral parlor, and providing Mod-demo, special forces' dog-and-pony show for visiting senators, congressmen, and foreign dignitaries.

Everyone hates Red Cycle because it takes up months of the year, and during that time you aren't doing anything remotely associated with special forces training. It is a wet wool blanket over the entire training year. Red Cycle made most of those in special forces consider quitting at one time or another.

Instead of stepping up the training and practice, Fort Bragg seemed stuck in place, and the trend was only getting worse. About a third of a group's forces are tied up in Red Cycle at any given time. The citizen-soldiers felt insulted. The idea was that they were going to hunt dangerous terrorists in the Horn of Africa, but rather than start training, they were spending their days clearing pine cones.

Red protested to the command sergeant major. He said sorry, those are the rules, for fully one-third of the group on Red Cycle. They were also starting to notice a distinct bias against the National Guard. He heard comments from the people in charge. They were calling them the "summer help." They were placed under operational control of 3rd Group, which meant they owned the unit, lock, stock, and barrel.

From that point, they were constantly being put first in line for the shitty details. First Battalion's commander gave Red the impression that he would throw someone under a truck in a second to cover his ass. Eye on the next promotion, check the block, move up, and kill anyone who gets in your way. The National Guardsmen were treated like the army's bastard stepchildren.

Soon it was April. Four months on active duty, and all they'd done was fill out forms, clear trash, and act on Mod-demo. The Horn of Africa was off, Afghanistan was on. Third Battalion of 3rd Special Forces Group went to relieve 5th SFGA. Alas, they were staying in 1st Battalion with nothing but Red Cycle as far as the eye could see.

The unit devised a plan of escape from Fort Bragg. Not desertion of course, but a sensible plan aimed at using their time efficiently rather than wasting it. They put together a plan to head out to the coast and do some maritime operations training. In their concept letter, they volunteered to head out to Key West to conduct the training in case they were called to a maritime theater of operations such as Somalia. That, too, was shot down, based on the fact it was Key West.

Their second choice for maritime operations training was the Fort Fisher Air Force Recreation Center north of Wilmington. The submission of their training plan, risk assessment, cost-and-expense work sheet, communications plan, and other paperwork, resembled an exercise in futility. Administrators would reject the submission based on form, which seemed to change from day to day, rather than content. Fucking madness. But amazingly, after a full three weeks, it was approved.

Once they got to Fort Fisher they stayed at a nice little cottage with one to two persons per room and settled in for a cool week at the beach. They had three boats, dry suits, wet suits, fins, masks, and snorkels. It was great fun, and Wilmington was close enough for them to drive out and get their drinks on in the evening.

Within a couple of days, the commander told them that the training was off. Everyone was to return to Fort Bragg. Bravo Company, 3rd Battalion, 20th SFGA, was being deployed to a still-secret location. At long last it looked like they were going to get a chance to play.

The next day Red and Captain Alan went to talk to the B-team. They parked the humvee and the trailer in the scuba locker parking lot. First, the commander briefed them on the first order of business: attach to 2nd Battalion and deploy to Afghanistan.

"Oh," the commander added, "but before that, we need to head up to Fort Pickett and do some training and an external evaluation to see if we're fit." Damn, thought Red and the captain. Why were they not training for war when they had the chance at Fort Bragg? Where were the regular army's priorities? Credit those jackasses for one thing—they sure knew how to waste time.

But the unit got over it, because the three-week training was helpful. First they went to the range and shot bullets. They conducted a day live-fire exercise then a night live-fire exercise. Everything was choreographed with the idea of "safety first." They prepared for a combat mission, a bullshit scenario in which they had to jump, walk a few kilometers, hit a complex of buildings, kill a terrorist known as Sa'ad, then run to a helicopter for exfil.

The "assault" started out pretty well. They approached the target with stealth, with the "objective rally point" just down the road. Another team had been radioing updates to them all the way up to their breaking out from their preassault position (last covered and concealed position) as they moved toward the objective. The other team had been on it, pulling special reconnaissance and real-time intel for about a day before they showed up.

The team's plan called for three separate elements to hit two buildings as a main effort, and the other team would clean up two buildings and look for squatters and such. Red's target was Green, the main effort. As they walked up the road in the assault element formations, they knew they were going to meet resistance, which they did. They laid down a barrage of fire, as Red smoked the crossroads and moved to objective Green.

Ringo was the breacher and had to place a simulated charge to blow the door. The simulation was made of some twine and wood, a piece of shit. Ringo was struggling to place the charge. In moments like these, time gets really slow. Red was pulling security for Ringo as he was fumbling with the charge, cursing like a sailor and sweating. Red kept saying, "Got to go, Ringo, let's go, Ringo." As he stood facing Ringo, the alarming thought crossed his mind that in a real-war situation, they would not have this kind of time. Recognizing this, they both burst into maniacal laughter.

The charge went off, and they flowed into the building just as they'd rehearsed. They found tons of intelligence and Sa'ad was "killed." Flipper was also killed, but then came back to life, and they all ran the full kilometer to the landing zone for mission pickup by "helicopters," which were really just trucks. The after-action review by 3rd SFGA observers was positive.

• • •

The team members went home for a few days and then back to Fort Bragg to pack and go. Red's wife "Lorie" had her sister "Wendy" and her two kids visiting. They planned to head down to the outer banks of North Carolina and rent a house for a week. Another friend of Lorie's and her kids were going to join them once they arrived. He was going to leave from the outer banks and head back to Fort Bragg before flying out.

Red drove down with his daughter, "Camille," to the beach house, with Lorie and Wendy a few hours behind in the minivan. The next days were full of family fun, warmth, lobsters, love, and the occasional birds-and-bees. "Max," who was two, was oblivious, but Camille was totally on to what was going on.

They spent the last day on Ockack Island walking around hand in hand, one family, Lorie to his right, holding Max's hand, and Camille to his left.

Then it was time. As they stood facing each other at the ferry landing, terrible thoughts crossed Red's mind. The sky was bright, and the air was pungent with myriad coastland smells. He thought he might never again see his wife, his adorable kids, this beautiful country. He might not survive his tour of duty.

Red climbed on the ferry, and his wife and children waved goodbye with tears streaming down their cheeks. Underneath a mask of coolness, he was deeply saddened.

CHAPTER **5**

# DEPLOYMENT

T here were no hurrahs in the plane, no war cries in anticipation of their long-delayed deployment, just dizziness and mind-numbing boredom. Finally they took off, stopped at Dover Air Force Base for five more hours, then flew on to the Rhein-Main Air Base near Frankfurt, Germany.

Germany was cool, a refreshing break in the boredom. With about 48 hours on the ground to fill, Red spent the first day looking around the base, the first night in Frankfurt with the team getting very drunk on Guinness, and the second day in bed farting and wishing he were dead. The team had gotten a little belligerent and a fistfight broke out. A good time all around.

Forty-eight hours later, they were on C-17s for the nine-hour flight to Kandahar. They got on board, popped their next round of sleeping pills, and were off to southern Afghanistan. The view from 20,000 feet was devoid of human life, of anything green, with mile after mile of tortured landscape, crossed with what looked like donkeys' trails, as far as the eye could see.

A few hours later, they landed at Kandahar Air Base. Consumed by the 110-degree heat of their new surroundings, Red blinked uncontrollably as he took his first look around. The earth was a slate gray, devoid of plant life, of anything green. It hadn't rained in southern Afghanistan for 14 straight years. Kandahar was once famous for its lush gardens, but the drought had turned them into a bowl of dust that billowed around vehicles as they moved about the airfield. A row of steep hills lined the horizon.

Afghanistan is really five distinct nations within a single political boundary. Afghans are not Arab; they are not Indian either. They are a collection of people of Aryan descent in the south and Mongol in the north. Although there has been some mixing of the races over time, the ethnic distinctions are quite obvious.

The largest ethnic group in Afghanistan is the Pashtun, of Aryan descent. They can be light skinned and may have green eyes. They occupy the entire southern half of the country and most of the areas along the eastern border. They speak Pushtu rather than the official language of the country, which is Dari or Farsi. Most Pashtun are from the Durrani or Ghilzai tribes. The Durrani occupy the area to the south, and the Ghilzai to the east. Red, Captain Alan, and the team were to operate exclusively among the Durrani.

To the north are the Tajik and the Hazara. They, too, have Aryan bloodlines, but they also have some Mongol mixed in. The Tajik and the Hazara speak Dari and have closer ties with Iran. Along the northern area of Afghanistan are the Turcoman ethnic groups: the Turkmen, the Tajik, and the Uzbek. All are ethnic Turco-Mongols.

To understand the war, you have to understand the ethnic divisions within Afghanistan. The Taliban were ethnic Pashtuns. Mullah Omar, leader of the Taliban, was a Durrani Pashtun. His capital was Kandahar. The Northern Alliance was made of the Turcoman groups, the Tajik, Uzbek, and Hazaras. Their capital, Kabul, sat on the line dividing the Pashtun from the Tajik.

Once the Taliban leadership fled into the hills, moderate Pashtun were placed in key leadership roles in the southern provinces. President Karzai was a Pashtun, as was King Zaher Shah, yet most of the levers in the interim government were held by the Tajik and Uzbeks. The Pashtun, who had dominated Afghanistan for hundreds of years, lost much of their economic and political power after the collapse of the Taliban.

The social structure in Pashtunistan can best be described as feudal. Each province is ruled by a governor. The Pashtun show extreme loyalty to their subclan, clan, and ethnic group. Disputes over such things as marriage can lead to blood feuds that are fought for generations.

The new central government has little authority over Pashtunistan. Pashtun warlords are most interested in their own personal power and wealth. If it's advantageous for them to support the Americans they will, but if it looks like the Taliban is winning, you'll see a lot of people who had just vowed to fight them to the death switch sides in a blink of an eye. Pashtun warlords have spent the last 25 years of civil war betraying each other on a daily basis.

The interaction of American forces with them would be defined by their position of power. The Pashtuns they were to deal with would look for weakness as an opportunity to exploit the situation. Red, Captain Alan, and most of the others were sensitive to their culture, and they stayed away from the population centers as best they could. They avoided the mosques, never spoke about religion, didn't drink alcohol with them, and never talked about women. As a rule, they maintained a sober and serious demeanor, avoided jokes, loud and impious behavior, and spoke only when necessary.

The ritual of meeting Pashtun leaders always begins with tea. It is considered polite to offer tea to visitors, so while many people respected and feared the Americans, they were offered and they drank a shitload (rather, *piss*load) of tea. Beast 85 bought a tea set so they, in turn, could offer tea to the tribesmen who visited them.

The Pashtuns' tea is uniquely green and strong. Rather than adding sugar to the tea, you put a sugar candy in your mouth, and the tea is sweetened as you drink it. After a brief handshake, followed by touching your chest as a gesture of respect, conversation would start over tea, or even a cold soda. Small talk would come first, then business, but it was not as ritualized as one might think.

• • •

Their tents at Kandahar Air Force Base were filthy. The green canvas had long since turned brown. About 20 people could cram into each tent, but they were given two tents per team, with about six guys per tent. No power generator sufficient to run the air conditioning was available, so the tents were hot, and when they were opened up to let air circulate, they became very dusty. The restrooms were portable johns, and they smelled really bad. It was a 15-minute walk just to shower.

The chow hall consisted of two large open tents next to the runway that served only MRE-type food—no fresh food to speak of. All the sections had generators, but no central electric grid for the base, so there was minimal refrigeration. Everything was served warm or hot. The problem was that all supplies were coming in by the air bridge from Germany; there are no sea ports close to Kandahar. The facilities in Kandahar were shitty, but in a few months the Kandahar Air Base would become a facility Beast 85 would look forward to visiting.

As soon as the team dropped their gear and got settled in, they started to look at the next jump. Prior to departing the States, the company commander had gone over roles the teams would use once in country. Their commander had been told that going into the deployment their company was going to pick up a majority of the battalion's support jobs in Bagram. This was couched as a "temporary thing," with other teams wanting to rotate in when the company was about to go into the "box," or isolate for a mission. This set off Beast 85's fine-tuned bullshit detectors. They knew it was simply about screwing the Guard once again.

One of the jobs that the B-team and one A-team needed to do was to shore up a logistics building at Bagram Airbase, called FOB–North. The 18th Airborne Corps was moving in, and the FOB North Building was a piece of prime real estate and the Combined Joint Special Operations Task Force (CJSOTF) wanted to keep it. There was no better way to do so than to occupy and improve it. The captain and Red wanted Beast 85 slotted for this task. It was the best way to get out of a support job. By proving they could hold together as a team on something so mundane and uninspiring, they were bound to be moved to their "higher calling"—combat—in no time at all. The captain pushed especially hard for it, and they got the job on the FOB North Building.

Their company was broken up as follows: six teams—Beast 80 to Beast 85—were placed in jobs as Area Specialty Teams (ASTs) working at the Special Forces Forward Operations Base or FOB 32, call sign Serpent 32. They were going to Bagram Airbase with Beast 80 (their B-team), which was given the job of setting up the building at Bagram. Beast 82 was coming with them.

The CJSOTF was being commanded by Colonel F., the 3rd Group commander, who was rumored to be on the edge of being relieved and replaced by Colonel S., the new 3rd Group commander. The story was that Colonel F. was being rotated early because of a leadership problem. Red listened to these rumors with half an ear. He thought that things would run more smoothly if the army were to fire half of all those above the rank of lieutenant colonel.

During their few days at Kandahar Airfield, Red attended a few commander's update briefings to get the lay of the land and learn how the war was progressing. He looked over the situational map and watched the role and position of the two other companies on the ground with 3rd SFGA. He began to formulate a few thoughts. Afghanistan is about the size of Texas. Some of the highest mountains on earth are in the north, and some of the hottest deserts in the world are in the south. Afghanistan has some of the toughest terrain on earth. They had two battalions of special forces deployed. Out of those two battalions there were maybe a total of 300 special forces guys in the field at any given time. The 101st Airborne Division had a brigade on the ground, but they were in Bagram and Kandahar Airfield for the most part. They went out on operations, but they typically stayed at the two airfields.

"Excuse me, sir," Red asked the commander, "what you're saying here is we have some 300 guns out there in a country the size of Texas with some of the hardest terrain on earth, and we're supposed to hunt down bin Laden and his 10,000 *mujaheedeen*. Am I missing something?"

The commander shook his head. No, apparently Red wasn't missing anything.

Third Battalion was gathering in Kandahar Airfield prior to its return to the States. These guys looked like they were back from the dead, all muscle, grist, and bones. They were skinny, had long hair and beards, had a nasty attitude, and held their chins high. They had been in the shit and they knew it. Red felt like a puppy in their presence.

They had been deployed along a section of mountainous territory that poked into Pakistan and was suspected of being the route the Taliban and al Qaeda used to move into Pakistan and back into Afghanistan. The teams were placed in firebases, local compounds rented to the American forces. The firebases would house a single team, or a B-team and a few teams, or a larger collection of 101st security guys, some CIA guys, and some Rangers with TF 11. From the firebases the team would react to missions directed from higher command, based on intelligence assets, or they would request missions to act on intelligence they developed locally.

C Company, under the direction of Major R., was attempting to convoy to an advanced operations base (AOB) south of the first company along the same border. They had been sitting at Kandahar Airfield for weeks waiting for helicopters to move the company into the field. The runway at Kandahar Airfield was lined with CH-47 utility helicopters that never seemed to move. The forward operations base commander was asking for helicopters because they didn't have any air assets organic to them. The 101st Airmobile division had lots of them. The FOB couldn't use them for some reason, so C Company sat on their asses. The CJSOTF commander didn't want to hear excuses and ordered the company to move to their AOB via ground convoy. This was the first of many examples Red saw of senior commanders making slapshot decisions without any tactical consideration. The convoy idea was insane. The terrain was treacherous, the roads impassable, and the logistics impossible. Like all good soldiers, they saluted the flag and headed out. A full third of the southern FOB's fighting forces was going to spend the next four weeks trying to make it to the AOB site before they had to turn around, but not before a few guys got killed.

Kandahar Airfield got rocketed a few times between 11 and 14 May. A guy from the 101st stepped on a mine and was seriously wounded. The tents were hot and dusty, and the weather grew hotter and hotter until the heat became intolerable. The men walked around like zombies. There were a few fistfights. The food was awful, and morale was poor.

Red went to the PX tent to buy some cigarettes. He noticed the tent's sides were suddenly being buffeted by a strong wind. He made his purchase and walked out of the tent. A huge, clearly demarked wall of dust hundreds of feet tall was just covering the runway. It was rushing toward Red. He ran. He got to his tent just as the wall of dust smashed into them. It was amazing. The tents were being punished. They closed every flap, but the dust poured in. The air in the tent was the color of brick. The dust was so fine that it was like powder when it settled on every surface. The dust storm passed in about 30 minutes, leaving a trail of dirt and destruction in its path. Everything that wasn't tied down was blown away. There was a rumble of thunder, and a few drops of mud fell from the sky.

# CHAPTER 6

# BAGRAM

Tuesday, 14 May—the B-team, 2082 (Beast 82), and Beast 85 got onto a C-17 flight to Bagram. The plane shot straight up in the air after takeoff, the engines screaming, the plane packed to the gills with gear, trucks, ISU90s (90-cubic-foot shipping containers), and men crammed in every available nook and cranny. The flight lasted about two hours. They flew north. The terrain had the same stark desolation Red saw a few days earlier on the way down: ruined towns, stunted orchards, and scabrous hills.

Two attack dogs rode along. They were in their little cages in the back of the plane, with Red in close proximity, and when the plane started up the dogs went apeshit. They spent the rest of the flight snapping and barking at everyone that walked by. There were a few humvees in the C-17. Red was looking at what he was going to have to do to climb up the side of the plane if those dogs busted out of their cages. They were sure giving it everything they had.

Approaching Bagram they ran into bad weather. Bagram lies about 40 miles north of Kabul, in a long, wide valley, surrounded on three sides by steep mountains. Red looked out the window of the C-17 and saw thick clouds with snow-covered mountains sticking out of them. The pilot told the men they were going to return to Kandahar. They were not going to try to land in the midst of a storm with all those big mountains around there. So they turned south and headed back.

Kandahar was the usual blast furnace, unbearably hot. The moment Red stepped on its soil he wished they'd stayed up north. What a contrast. Afghanistan is like that: freezing temperatures in the mountains up north, scorching desert down south. They kept their gear in the departure area run by the air force and walked back to the FOB area to try again the next day.

Early the next day they got into a C-130, and like the C-17 the day before, it was filled with vehicles and massive containers (ISU90s). The C-130 struggled into the air and headed north. The flight was slower and bumpy. Flying in an overloaded air force aircraft in bad weather, particularly in a combat zone, is not a lot of fun.

Four hours later, they landed at Bagram Airbase under clear skies. The crew chief lowered the tailgate as they taxied toward the loading ramp. Red walked out onto the ramp and looked out. Bagram was unbelievably verdant. The mountains surrounding the airfield were covered with snow. The breeze was cool.

A B-team guy that had flown up a week before met them at the arrival ramp. The walk from the departure area was short, only about two blocks from the arrival ramp. The airfield was filled with CH-47s, A-10s, and MH-60s. There were a lot of people running around. The compound was straight down the road from the departure area, across the main road.

The "Bagram Hyatt Resort" offered quite deluxe accommodations: a roof that had been blown off, plaster riddled with bullet holes, whole sections of walls missing, and a large mess hall with a front room partitioned with plywood. It had been occupied by the 5th Special Forces Group when they first moved into the valley with the Northern Alliance a few months earlier. The main building was surrounded by a bunch of tents and a smaller building that had probably been a bakery. The team was given a tent to live in at first and then moved into the main building when a 3rd Group team left for a firebase.

The CJSOTF was across a small road from their compound. Red couldn't see the entire thing from his first vantage, but it sure looked big. Some of the guys bunking there warned them to stay away from the area because the officers and senior NCOs were starting to make a big deal about facial hair and general cleanliness. To them, Beast 85 must have looked like a regular rogue's gallery, filthy and unshaven. It was like a casting call for a "Dirty Dozen" remake.

One big event looming on the horizon was the arrival of Lieutenant General McNeal, the 18th Airborne Corps three-star general who was coming to command the entire task force in Afghanistan. Lots of guys with the "puking dragon," another name for the 18th Airborne Corps patch, were milling around. Beast 85 set up a perimeter around the compound to keep the 18th Airborne Corps guys away from their prized real estate.

The command structure of Afghanistan looked like this:
Lieutenant General McNeal—18th Airborne Corps
    Commander.
In charge of one brigade of infantry, lead by a colonel.
A CJSOTF, commanded by a colonel, in charge of two SF
    battalions and the coalition Special Operations
    Forces (SOF).
McNeal's staff, more than 500 strong.
The CJSOTF staff, more than 300 strong.

The FOB's staff was composed of about 30 people.
There were maybe 300 guys in the field at any given time.

As always in the army, the staff-to-fighter ratio was huge. Generals demanded to make decisions that would be better left to a captain or major in the field. For their purposes, the men of Beast 85 were warned to stay away from the three-ring circus of CJSOTF. They filed haircut profiles (HCPs), or permission requests to grow beards and long hair. They spent entire days doing nothing but growing their beards and desperately trying to avoid airborne command staff, who were bored, numerous, and seemed more concerned with the men's appearance than conducting the war itself. It really was a three-ring circus.

Red walked over to the CJSOTF one day to take a look and to get on the access roster to attend a few of the commander's update briefings, to get a better understanding of the war's progress. The CJSOTF compound was named after the recently retired command sergeant major (CSM) of 3rd SFGA—a drunk and, in Red's opinion, an asshole, so he fit in well with the rest of the CSMs.

A number of brick buildings, in addition to three prefab tents, housed the entire CJSOTF staff. The operations tent took up an area of about 200 by 400 feet, and was about 20 feet tall. It had air conditioning, carpet, and a white liner. The space was filled with desk after desk of busy staff officers. At least they looked busy. There were all kinds of eager-beaver clerks running around, all of them properly shaved with good military haircuts and proper uniforms. After seeing the size of the staff operation, Red thought it must be so large because they were supporting such a big war effort. There were fewer than 300 guys in the field.

The team began to wear civilian clothing, confusing the CJSOTF staff. They didn't know if the men were CIA, CAG, CI, or E-I-E-I-O. As long as they were kept guessing, they left the men alone. Beast 85 took advantage of the opportunity to sneak out of the compound for lunch and dinner. Headquarters food was great, unlike the shit special forces guys were eating down south. Steaks, plenty of fruit and fresh vegetables, fresh milk, and ice cream. Red supposed the reason the food was so good was because headquarters needed fuel for its excess brainpower.

Then came the commander's update briefing, which included the missions of their friends in the 19th SFGA. Red paid extra-close attention. He soon realized that the same missions were being presented over and over again. The missions in Kandahar represented what was going on in the entire country—only five SF companies and not nearly enough guns. They were told there was a shortage of helicopters. That didn't jibe with their own observations. The airfield was covered with CH-47 Chinooks, and they had talked to the helicopter crews, who said their birds were fine. Like Red and the rest of the gang, they were looking for action.

They knew the Taliban forces were regrouping. They were getting bolder by the day, staging ambushes across the country. Meanwhile, Beast 85's own leaders were tying the team's hands, not letting them fight the war they came to fight. Instead, the entire company was relegated to staff work. The staff was already huge, and it was growing bigger, without a single man being added to field operations. Red started to hum that tune you hear at the circus, the one that signals the entry of the clowns.

So the men directed their hostilities and frustrations toward improving the compound. They found huge steel squares that might once have housed filters. They welded them together to create a screen around the compound. They added prefab sandbag barriers along other parts of the perimeter. They improved the water system, built an ammunition supply point, and picked up tons of trash.

Ten days into their stay at the Bagram Circus, one of the company's teams, Beast 84, was given the job of heading to the field with a 3rd Group team. Usually when A-teams deploy into firebases, they bring troops from the 101st or the 82nd Airborne to provide local security. This allows the teams to concentrate their time and resources in the wild yonder.

But this time, the 3rd Group team couldn't get a platoon from the 101st, and didn't trust Afghans for firebase security. They were ready to head out, so Beast 84 was assigned to provide security. They would be the first from their company to get into the field. Red was jealous.

They deployed to Bagram with the 3rd Group teams and started getting the vehicles and equipment ready for the helicopter trip to Lawara, a small village along the Pakistani border. They put on their war kit and headed to the airfield. CH-47s, which were available for some reason, were sling-loading the humvees and Toyota trucks along with a full complement of team guys and gear in four helicopters, which would make three lifts over three days to move everyone to Lawara and the new firebase. It was an exciting time for the guys of Beast 84.

Like the captain and the rest of the guys, Red was as determined as ever to get into the mix, and soon. Call him crazy, but he wanted action—real action. Beast 85 was ready, chomping at the bit. A smart commander would have deployed them right then and there. Instead, here they were, their thumbs up their asses cleaning up a damn advanced operations base (AOB).

Throughout their time in Bagram, only a few things struck Red as worthwhile, one of which was the consumption of a fair amount of beer alongside Her Majesty's Royal Marines, who could really put it down. Also, there was a Spanish hospital near Bagram that had a lot of pretty nurses. Otherwise, it was boring as hell.

If they lingered much longer, an AST might switch with them, probably splitting up the team into various staff duties in the process. That would suck shit.

The team looked for ways to help their cause. Their hopes hinged on their one "connection"—a chief warrant officer in the future plans section of the CJSOTF. They asked him to keep Beast 85 in mind the next time they considered assets to move.

Then in late May they were asked by the CJSOTF to fly to the firebase in Shkin to pick up three members of the local AMF (Afghan military force). Something very strange had happened there about a week earlier. Their team was on a recon mission as part of Operation Mountain Lion when they were ambushed by Taliban fighters. The convoy was halfway through some pinch terrain when an Afghan walked up to one of the Toyota Hilux pickup trucks, pulled a kalashnikov out from under his shawl, and fired two rounds point-blank into the chest of 19th Group SOTA Sergeant Gene Arden Vance Jr. from West Virginia.

One of the team members on an ATV behind the Hilux hopped off, walked up to the Taliban, and killed him almost point-blank. Then they tried to resuscitate Sergeant Vance. The air medical evacuation helicopter took over three hours to come in. They were too late, and Sergeant Vance died. He was 38, recently married, and had canceled his honeymoon plans when he was called up to serve in Afghanistan. Mountain Lion was an extensive operation designed to locate, isolate, and destroy al Qaeda and Taliban fighters. There were no excuses not to have a medevac bird ready at Bagram Airfield during Operation Mountain Lion. It could have saved Sergeant Vance's life.

The ensuing investigations determined that three people—a translator, an AMF officer, and a soldier—had acted suspiciously. It was thought that they might have some involvement with the enemy. A helicopter was to come and pick them up and bring the suspects back to Bagram as "persons under control," or PUCs, for a formal interrogation. The three guys had not been told that they were under suspicion. The story they were told was that the Americans in Bagram wanted to talk to them about the details of the ambush.

Red volunteered himself for the mission, along with four other guys from Beast 85. It was their first mission, and they loaded for bear: one-and-a-half times the standard load for Red's M4, same for the pistol, radios, grenades, and personnel deterrent munitions—everything he could carry on his body armor.

Rock, Flipper, Bubble Boy, T.T. Boy, and Red all met at the airfield at the appointed time, about 0900. They were to fly out to the area of operations (AO) Cougar firebases, drop a few guys off, deliver mail, and then swing into Shkin to grab their "friends."

The flight was with two UH-60 Black Hawks fitted with external fuel tanks, flown by the 101st Airborne. Rock was a cop in civilian life, so Red was going to let him handle the handcuffing and searching of the suspects. The mission briefing was unclear, and they were not exactly sure what to expect.

Bagram was under a 180-day desert wind that would last from mid-June to late December. The base would remain under a cloud of very fine dust all the time. The dirt got into your eyes, your mouth, everything, but mostly your eyes.

The two UH-60s lifted off from Bagram at 1000 hours and headed southeast. Bagram is in a huge horseshoe valley with the Panshir on one end and Kabul and the plains to the south on the other. Southeast toward Pakistan, the border was porous. These mountains could get quite high, but nothing like the high alpine mountains of 18,000-plus feet to the north. The doors in the aircraft were open. There were door gunners in the left and right crew seats with M60 machine guns. Red was given a headset to communicate with the crew and could hear the pilots talking between themselves and over the radio to each other. As they approached the mountains, the pilots avoided the high ground and stuck to the valleys and draws. The scenery during the flight was spectacular.

As they moved into the valleys, the UH-60s flew between the ever-growing hills and gorges. The mountains were mostly brown rock with small hard shrubs spread out here and there. Red's helicopter was in the lead.

They followed a draw between and up to a crest in a row of mountains, popped up over the crest, and dove down into the valley below at 45 degrees. They flew into dusty plains and got so close to the ground that the rotor wash blew dust up and behind them as they roared over small villages. The people ran out of their homes and looked upon the low-flying choppers in amazement.

The guys were doing over a hundred miles per hour, but an AK-47 could have easily hit them. Red was trying to be alert and scan the side of the bird for threats, but he kept finding himself distracted and amazed at the rugged beauty of the terrain below.

DEPARTMENT OF THE ARMY
HEADQUARTERS, 3d SPECIAL FORCE GROUP (AIRBORNE)
FORT BRAGG, NORTH CAROLINA 28310

ORDERS 3DSFG 04-053                      30 April 2002

GROUP ORDER – SEE ATTACHED – MAINBODY, 2ⁿᵈ BN, 3d SFG (A) (WHQMTO), FORT BRAGG, NORTH CAROLINA 28310

You are reassigned and/or deployed as shown below and are to return to your permanent station upon completion of the duties in support of this operation. You will submit a reviewed travel voucher for this travel to the finance office within 5 working days after returning to home station.

Temporary reassignment to: B Co 2ⁿᵈ BN 3d SFG (A) FORWARD (WHQMA1) APO AE 09354 (QATAR) USCENTCOM AOR
Purpose of temporary duty: ISO OPERATION ENDURING FREEDOM
Number of days: 179 days with possible extension to 364 days.
Will Proceed date: O/A 12 May 02 from homestation.
Security Clearance: See attached/verified by 3ᴿᴰ SFG (A) GRP S-2, DSN 239-4136.
Acct class: 9720100.56SA 0 50 5092 012173.63000 21T1/21T2 000000 CAH3306TG04053
UEIS8 S31007
Project Code: 9GF; MDEP: X063; FCA: F3202; F3203; F3204
Movement designator code: PME2/FMO2
Authority: VOCO CDR USASOC
Additional instructions: (a) You are deployed in a TCS status. This is not a Permanent Change of Station (PCS). Normal PCS entitlements, allowances and relocation of family members are not authorized. (b) During period of deployment, deployed unit commander has responsibility for personnel service support to include awards and decorations, personnel strength accounting, UCMJ, and all other forms of personnel and legal administration support except reserve component promotion authority. (c) Containerized weapons are authorized for commercial travel; classified documents will be transported incident to travel. (d) Soldier Readiness Processing (SRC) will be accomplished prior to departure from losing installation/home station per AR 600-8-11. (e) Variations authorized Germany, Egypt, Kuwait, Bahrain, and Qatar, Pakistan, Oman, Uzbekistan, and Afghanistan. (f) Personnel should depart with sufficient funds to pay for meals/billeting en-route (in flight meals/government meals directed). Government quarters and mess is available and directed. (g) Family Separation Allowance-II (FSA-II) is payable to all soldiers with dependents who are deployed 31 consecutive days or longer. Hardship Duty Pay for location (HDP-L), is authorized for enlisted soldiers and officers for Kuwait, Bahrain, Afghanistan, Qatar, Uzbekistan and Oman. Hostile Fire/Imminent Danger Pay (HF/IDP) authorized in Kuwait, Bahrain, Oman, Afghanistan and Qatar. Combat Zone Tax Exclusion (CZTE) is authorized. Upon returning to home station, soldier should complete DA Form 1351-2 and submit to servicing finance office in conjunction with a finalized travel voucher. (h) Rental cars are authorized in the event government transportation is not available or conducive to mission accomplishment.

---

ORDERS 04-053     HQ, 3d SFG (A) & FT BRAGG, NC 28310     30 April 2002

(i) Commercial lodging and local per diem rate are authorized if no government quarters are available. Statement of non availability is required. (j) Meals and incidentals are authorized while in transit (k) ARCENT-CJTF per diem $3.50 a day (l) Basic Allowance for Housing (BAH) is based upon their permanent duty station. (m) Soldier will retain BAS, if applicable. (n) Each deployed soldier will be reported as deployed within the SIDPERS SYSTEM. (o) Excess baggage authorized 200lbs. (p) Airborne operations authorized. (q) Official phone calls authorized. (r) Foreign flag carrier authorized.

FOR THE COMMANDER:

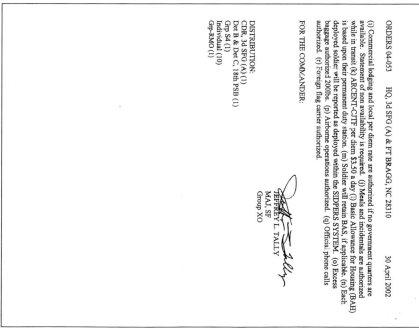

JEFFREY L. TALLY
MAJ, SF
Group XO

T.T. Boy sleeping like a baby at Fort Pickett in April 2002.

Rock, Bubble Boy, and Mongo in the van headed to the ranges at Fort Pickett in April 2002.

May 2002: The entire team at the range outside of Bagram Airfield, from left to right. Top row: Bubble Boy, Kev, T.T. Boy, Ringo, the captain, Red, Mongo. Bottom row: Flipper, Rock, Stitch, Doc Hoss.

May 2002: Beast 85 at the range. They would drive into the desert and shoot into the side of a mountain. They were able to go to the range a few times to maintain their skills.

May 2002: Rock at the Forward Operations Base (North).

May 2002: A caravan of nomadic Kuchies passes the range.

May 2002: T.T. Boy watching the vehicle with a crowd of locals around him. Everywhere they went, crowds of locals wanted to check them out.

May 2002: The company commander buys an old Martini Henry Rifle on Chicken Street, Kabul.

May 2002: A store in Kabul selling the humanitarian aid gifts to the Afghans. Most of the aid ended up on the black market.

May 2002: The wrecks of the Afghan air force, destroyed on the ground, were moved into piles between the runways at Bagram Airfield.

May 2002 at the Forward Operations Base (North). This was the staging and deployment site for TF 32 at Bagram Airbase. Beast 85 was sent here to build a wall around it.

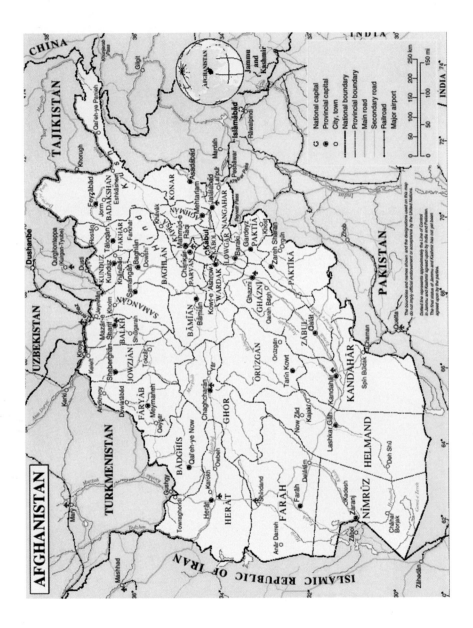

May 2002: The ruins of the American International School of Kabul. Red was a student there as a young boy from 1969 to 1970.

May 2002: Darlaman Palace was the king's residence and was later used as government buildings. It was in pretty bad shape as is clear in this photo.

Happiness is a belt-fed weapon: Doc Ken and Rock outside one of the Toyota trucks on the way to the Helmand River valley (Operation Full Throttle).

The terrain on the way to Deh Rawod (Operation Full Throttle).

Coming down the mountains into the Helmand River valley.

Kandahar was once a green, tree-filled city. The mostly dry canals fill with water once every two months.

Red, on the way to Deh Rawod (Operation Full Throttle).

Spidey was injured as he dove for cover when machine-gun and hand-grenade fire swept the compound in Tarin Kowt. Spidey had to get stitched up, but he was OK.

Bubble Boy relaxing at the firebase in Deh Rawod.

The firebase in Deh Rawod had a fountain, perfect for a swim if you don't mind bacteria. Left to right: Ringo, Stitch (back), Rock, Spidey, Kev, and a guy from the 3rd Group team.

Clear-air tornados would roll around on the dry flats. Although they couldn't pull a human off their feet, they would make a mess of the base camp. They would rise up to hundreds of feet high and would roll around for hours.

When the local warlord came to visit them at Deh Rawod, he would bring his bodyguards, thugs like the ones above who had fought for the Taliban a few months earlier.

Rock and Ringo in the marijuana field. As cops in America, they could only imagine making a bust on such a crop.

A rare cloudy day. The landscape around the Helmand River valley was quite fantastic. Stitch is standing on the armored humvee as they move to investigate the village across the river.

Rock at the end of the trail to the objective (Operation Full Throttle).

They continued on for about an hour, climbing ever higher into the mountains. Red heard the pilot say the border with Pakistan was a few miles off the port side of the bird. It was getting very rugged. Steep hills with deep valleys and gorges marching north to south passed under them. To the east, and toward Pakistan, the mountains grew in height. As always, the sky was bright clear and blue. Other than the occasional truck or bus they encountered, if they had gone back in time a thousand years, the scene below would have been the same.

Their first stop was Uruzgan firebase. The compound was a collection of walled adobe buildings and tents surrounded by barbed wire. It was in a large valley running north to south in a valley between two high mountain ridges. The firebase dominated the plain with humvees, bunkers, antennas, people in desert camouflage, and what looked like a mortar pit. There were a few adobe compounds farther up the valley, but the area was isolated. Two dirt roads intersected at the firebase.

They landed just outside the wire. These trips were the only ticket out of the area. It was first come, first served on the return trip, no waiting list. They dropped off lots of mail, a few guys, and told the people who wanted to get on right then and there that they were going to be back in about an hour or so. Red was hearing all of this on the headset. He was told Shkin would be the next stop.

They lifted off again and headed south. Red started growing concerned at this point. If the PUCs were not going to cooperate, then the team would have to hog-tie them and secure them to the floor of the aircraft. It could mean that an American who merely wanted a flight home would have to give up their space on the bird, and would have to wait a week until the next flight to Bagram. Red relayed his concerns to the crew. They said they would support him if it came to him having to kick everyone off who was not part of the PUC pickup.

Shkin was in a valley that seemed much wider than the others. The valley floor looked green, and there was a large mountain stream following the side of the first ridge of mountains. What looked like birch trees were growing along the side of the stream. They passed over the firebase, which was another adobe compound, and then circled around to land upwind and closer to a collection of humvees that were gathered in a field.

They landed, and Red got out of the helicopter and walked toward the team members standing around the humvee. He asked them for the whereabouts of the team sergeant, and they pointed him instead to the team commander. He told Red the team sergeant was off on a mission, but that he wanted to brief him on how the PUC pickup was going down.

There was to be no appearance that this was an arrest, at least until they left the compound. The Afghans in their local force were not to see the suspects being handcuffed and roughed up. Otherwise, they'd have a revolt on their hands. Red agreed to the team commander's request. He gave Red a stack of papers in an envelope—interrogation notes and background documentation on the three PUCs.

Red grabbed the PUCs and moved them toward the helicopter. He patted them down and searched through their stuff for weapons or explosives. Then he told Rock, who was assisting him, to play it cool. The three suspects were separated and took their seats in the helicopter. A team member sat across from them with orders to kill them if they threatened the aircraft. The Afghans were freaked out about flying. They began to sweat in the cool air.

They left Shkin and headed back to Uruzgan. Upon arrival, they loaded up on fuel and stuffed as many people in the bird as it could hold, and off they went. The three-hour flight back to Bagram wasn't very thrilling, high and flat above the terrain.

As they approached the arrival ramp, Red asked the crew to drop the passengers off and then taxi to a secluded area, shut down, and wait for the CJSOTF's welcome party to pick up the PUCs and place them in custody.

They waited for 40 minutes. Finally, a CIA guy drove up and said he was sorry for keeping them waiting. He was medium-built, lean, and well shaven. He struck Red as the analyst type. The agent told him to wait because he had not yet arranged to have the PUCs transported to the interrogation facility. He left and returned with a tough-looking pair of MPs and another humvee. The PUCs were told to kneel and place their hands behind their head. They were surprised, but they did as they were told. Red and the agent left to drop off the paperwork and sign the PUCs into the interrogation facility.

The agent walked Red to the interrogation center, which was a large building located along the flight line. It was a nondescript place you might walk by a thousand times and never notice. They continued through the back door and up a flight of stairs. The upper deck had a banister that overlooked the large open floor below. With its 35-foot ceilings, it had to have something to do with aircraft maintenance, except there were no hangar doors to be seen. Along the far wall was a line of cages, and in those cages were Taliban and al Qaeda prisoners.

Red dropped the files the team commander had given him and asked to leave. He also asked for and received a 12-pack of beer for his trouble.

The remainder of their time in Bagram was spent cleaning up the AOB building. The 18th Airborne Corps was moving into Bagram in force, and they had hundreds of staff officers, all looking about as fearsome as an 18-year-old math major, wandering around demanding they be saluted. Red was desperate to leave.

Beast 85's CJSOTF connection tried his best to help. The team was considered for three more missions that they knew of, but each one was canceled at the last minute for one reason or another. One involved a mission to the Konar Valley north of Jalalabad with the 19th SFGA, a group committed to putting forces in the field.

The CJSOTF wanted to put a team in a firebase in the town of Asadabad, 70 miles up the donkey trail from civilization. They asked Beast 85 if they wanted the job. The men jumped up and yelled, "Hell, yes!" Finally, it looked like they were going to war.

But two strong factors worked against them. First, 19th Group already had the team guys necessary for the mission. They mostly needed a team with vehicles to throw at the firebase. Unfortunately, Beast 85 didn't have them.

The biggest factor working against them, bigger than their lack of vehicles, was their company commander, Major B. He was determined to command an AOB and do great things for his country. He was a smart commander who understood that the war was starting to be led by clowns, and the opportunity to fight was now or never.

Major B. had three of his five teams pulling staff duty, one team providing security for "real" A-teams, and one team putting up a fence at the compound in Bagram. Beast 85's trip up the Konar Valley would transfer their operational control to 19th Special

Forces Group (Airborne). The major was against the transfer. He didn't want to see the team go, at least not without him.

Red couldn't blame him for his good sense. Beast 85 was the strongest team. Major B. was a good commander and wanted to do what all good commanders would do—head into the fight with his best men. In addition, the only way he was going into the combat zone was by leading Beast 85's company. He knew it, and he didn't want to lose the team. He did his damnedest to convince the FOB commander not to transfer them out from under him.

Eventually, the CJSOTF commander came around to his side. He retracted the order attaching Beast 85 to 19th SFGA. So they were scratched from the mission and went back to clearing trash.

A second opportunity came from the CIA, of all places. They wanted a team of special forces guys to move to Kabul and work with a small group of Afghans to arm, train, and lead into battle a special operations team. If selected, Beast 85 would get a group of motivated, educated Afghans and teach them special operations techniques and procedures. This would allow Afghans to take care of their own business. The CIA and special forces had developed a close working relationship early in the war. They quickly learned to rely on the SF teams to provide security for themselves and to help them exploit a target when the opportunity arose.

Beast 85 jumped at the chance. Red knew for a fact that if they started to work with the CIA they would be out of sight of the CJSOTF, and they would have a real chance of getting some trigger time. Alas, Major B. said no.

But then an operations base in the Helmand River valley in the south-central part of the country began picking up intelligence that something was going on in the town of Deh Rawod, the childhood home of Taliban leader Mullah Omar.

Deh Rawod was an isolated town about 150 miles north of Kandahar. The Helmand River runs from the central mountains west of Kabul due south into the desert, where it disappears into the sand. The river is the sole source of water in many parts of the country, including Deh Rawod.

The valley formed by the Helmand River is also one of the largest opium poppy growing regions on earth. The river runs through Uruzgan province, Kandahar province, and Helmand province. The Taliban got its start in this region as a militia, protecting convoys traveling between Pakistan and central Asia from local warlords, eventually seizing control of 90 percent of the country. Three high-level terrorists—the three highest-ranking Taliban—were all known to be hiding somewhere in this valley: Mullah Osmani, Mullah Barader, and Mullah Omar himself.

The coalition SOF teams from Norway, Germany, Australia, and Canada had been running around up in the mountains surrounding the town and were coming under fire when their helicopter flew over the town. It was assumed that the antiaircraft fire was directed at the helicopters to protect persons of interest in the Deh Rawod area. SIGINT was picking up phone calls and phone numbers that correlated with persons of interest. Special recon teams started to watch the town, and SIGINT people started to listen a little closer. The FOB commander was thinking about sending some of his boys up into the valley and start shaking the tree.

Beast 85 got the call. The captain flew to Kandahar for a briefing, and the rest of the team started to pack. No more of this stinking cleanup duty. No staff work. They were going into the shit.

First, the team was given a little cash to play with—a $50,000 operational fund, plus a couple hundred thousand Pakistani rupees for day-to-day necessities. They were going to do a little "shopping" in Kabul.

They were authorized to buy anything they thought they needed; that is, except weapons, of which they had an ample supply, and vehicles, which they were to rent. Ringo and Steve ("Stitch") were appointed team purchasing officer and team fund officer, respectively. Red had some trepidation about two people controlling so much dough, but Ringo and Stitch kept meticulous records, and both were honest to the bone.

The company commander gave his own stamp of approval to the shopping spree, provided he could come along. On top of operational fund resources, he wanted a carpet and an antique gun.

The team also brought along the perfect tour guide, a U.S. Air Force terminal air controller named Sam who had been hanging around the AOB. He had earlier become acquainted with some Kabul locals who sold carpets. He had worked with 5th group teams, and would watch their back and make sure they weren't screwed on the prices.

Kabul was a 45-minute drive south of Bagram. As this was still Tajik country, the road was safe. However, the city itself was in bad shape. Entire sections were in ruins, with roofs blown off and walls riddled with myriad bullet holes. The team drove past the U.S. Embassy—"the fort," as it was known. The CIA and other government agencies occupied a compound across from the Afghan parliament building and the Araania Hotel. They had stacked 20-foot sea containers around the compound, building a huge wall for protection. The street through downtown, Chicken Street (the fabled hippie road to Kathmandu and a bazaar for carpets, muskets, swords, armor, snakes—you name it), was closed to vehicle traffic and guarded by hulking DynCorp and Blackwater security contractors.

This was not Red's first time in Kabul. Not by a long shot. In fact, he had last visited it in 1979, when his family lived in Pakistan, just as the Russians were preparing to invade. As a child, he lived in Kabul for four years. His family's neighborhood had been an upscale residential area known as Charti-Kar, where many other international families resided. His memories of Charti-Kar were of a large central road, Darlaman Boulevard, with trees on both sides, stretching to the old King's Palace at the far end.

In the marketplace the team bought two portable generators, some cooking stuff, lanterns, blankets, local clothing, water filtration cisterns, and smaller items like batteries. So far, Red found Kabul to be the same charming, colorful, busy place he remembered.

On the team's next visit to town, they went looking for Red's family's old house in Charti-Kar, not knowing quite what to expect. He remembered the area as very green, but alas, when they turned down the boulevard past the Kabul Zoo, it was not the vista he remembered. It was total destruction. Two blocks into Darlaman the houses were leveled. Skeletons of structures poked up here and there. There were no more trees left. The landscape was denuded. Darlaman was pockmarked with shell craters. The palace at the end of the road had been severely damaged.

Red recognized a few landmarks and directed Ringo to take a right at a street near the river. The buildings were all knocked down. Two blocks later, on the left, there it was—his old house. It was in bad shape. The team stopped outside and got out of the vehicle to inspect the damage. It had taken a grenade or two, the front was riddled with bullet holes, and the whole thing was fire-damaged.

The arrival of Americans in any part of town always drew a crowd, which looked at them as if they were from Mars. A kid in rags stared out at Red from behind the hole in the wall from his old house. The guy from the carpet store, who was acting as the team's translator, explained to the crowd that Red had lived in the house many years ago as a child. He relayed back to Red that a caretaker was watching the place and that the owners lived in New York. Red took some pictures and drove off to look for the American International School of Kabul where he went to kindergarten and first grade.

The team turned back up Darlaman toward the palace. The roof was gone. Most of the buildings were flattened. Red was about to jump the wall, but a kid warned him that the area was mined.

The translator told them that after the Russians left the city the rival Afghan warlords fought over Kabul for years. There were government buildings in Charti-Kar, and the downtown area was sheltered by hills, so thousands of 122mm rockets were fired at Kabul, and most of them landed in Charti-Kar. Red snapped a few more digital pictures and split.

On the last trip Red took into Kabul he was to orient the leadership of two platoons from SEAL Team 1 on the areas surrounding Kabul. The Loya-Jurga, or grand council, was coming up, and they wanted to make sure that Beast 85 was ready to jump into any fight that might start up. The Loya-Jurga was a collection of tribal elders from across the country who were going to come together and give President Karzai legitimacy to rule the country until 2004. This was their first meeting in three decades of civil war. The SEALs were told to expect the expression of some hard feelings between the participants, including possible gun battles between feuding warlords and assassination attempts.

The two Platoons from SEAL Team 1 moved into Beast 85's compound. They were 25,000 miles from the nearest ocean, and the stuff they were doing was not a textbook SEAL mission. But they had lobbied hard to get into the game, so here they were.

When they showed up Red was a little leery of having them as compound mates. SEALs have a reputation for being hopelessly vain, belligerent, and unable to back up their talk with action. The average SEAL was 10 to 12 years younger than the members of Beast 85 and were not as cohesive a group. Part of this has to do with the nature of the assignments: the classic SEAL mission is in-and-out, whereas when special forces go in, they stay in, giving them plenty of time to bond.

The orientation trip took them around the city to valleys and hills that were considered strategic in value and might afford the Taliban the vantage they needed to launch a rocket or two. This trip would end up being Red's last into his former home of Kabul.

# CHAPTER 7

# KANDAHAR

Red would never again see Bagram. From this point forward, for the rest of the team's deployment, they would be "in the box." The adventure was about to begin.

They flew back to Kandahar in a C-130 on 11 June with all of their stuff packed into large shipping containers. The aircraft was overloaded, and it took the entire runway to take off. Red was looking out one of the small windows of the plane as it slowly lumbered down the runway. He watched as the markers slowly ticked off, and he lifted into the air at the last marker. He could feel the plane struggling to gain altitude and speed. It would be a damned shame if, after all this waiting around, they all died trying to get off the ground. Red looked around the aircraft and saw that everyone else was sleeping or not acting concerned. The flight was horrible.

But they made it. The captain met them at the arrival area. They loaded into a light medium tactical vehicle and drove a half mile to the forward operating base. Captain Alan moved some of Beast 84's stuff out of one tent and into another so they could have two tents together for themselves and their gear. They had no idea at the time that there would be lingering resentment toward them because they "kicked" Beast 84 out of that tent.

They had no sooner unpacked some of their gear, grabbed a shower, and eaten dinner when a runner from the base came out and said that Red and Captain Alan were wanted immediately in the Operations Center (OPCEN). They were going to receive a warning order, meaning there was a chance they were going to pick up a mission on the spot.

The captain knew it was a race between Beast 85 and another team from 3rd Group on who could redeploy back to Kandahar quickest. Half of the 3rd Group team had returned, and they had the mission. The other half was going to be flying in that night. They were already planning for an infiltration into the Helmand province to set up a blocking position to support a sweep up the valley by another team.

The future operations officer met with Red and the captain in the planning cell and told them that the MC-130, code name "Chariot 55," had crashed on takeoff from a small airstrip along the Pakistani border and was burning. It was not clear if anyone had survived, but the foregone conclusion was that most of the people on board perished. Beast 65 was out of the game. Beast 85 was to take their place on the mission.

The reason why the 3rd Group team was pulled out of the field in such a hurry for a two-day mission was a mystery. Beast 85 was sitting in Bagram free and clear. Although they were told it was "a race between us and them," it never made sense that it was a race at all, unless you lived the life of a National Guard team assigned to 3rd Special Forces Group. They wanted their boys in the game whether it made sense or not. Beast 85 was there as a contingency if Beast 65 was unable to make it. In the end, they overloaded an MC-130 in their rush to leave the field, and the plane was unable to gain altitude and crashed. Kind of spooky. Beast 85 could easily have suffered the same fate in their earlier rush to return to Kandahar with an overloaded plane.

Following the warning order, the men were given a briefing on the situation. The FOB was going to conduct a sweep-and-destroy mission up the Helmand River valley, and through Deh Rawod. Beast 85 and another 3rd Group team were to infil into the valley earlier that night and set up two blocking positions. One was to the north of Deh Rawod in the Helmand River valley, and the other was in a major gully that provided an easy avenue for entry or escape. Beast 85 was going to set up the blocking position in the gully. They were to capture or destroy any "squirters" that might be running into the valley or away from the two teams pushing up the valley.

The reason that Beast 85 was inserting into this valley was because, for the previous two weeks, every aircraft that had over-flown the area of Deh Rawod had received ground fire: 23mm antiaircraft fire, 12.7mm DShK ("dushka") rounds, either of which could easily take down a low-flying aircraft. They were part of a bigger picture. Once they and another team to the north were in place, two additional teams would push up from the south in their vehicles.

The current enemy made a practice of moving away from decisive contact with U.S. forces in favor of harassing attacks at a time and place of their own choosing. In accordance with this assessment, the plan supposed that any truly bad guys would receive an advance warning because of their relatively sophisti-cated early warning system, then move along the road and trail networks to the north to avoid the approaching armed vehicles sweeping in from the south.

Beast 85 would identify and engage them in a pre-positioned ambush site benignly referred to in the operations order as a "roadblock." They were to infiltrate into the northern Helmand province of Afghanistan, about 20 kilometers northwest of Deh Rawod.

There were only two major roads exiting to the north from the Deh Rawod area, and there were special forces A-teams with attached indigenous forces blocking both of them. They would be the net to catch the bad guys.

The men had just over 24 hours before the helicopters were going to lift off. Red and the captain went over the sequence of events.

The team must have known something was going on, because by the time Red got to the tents, they had already assembled. He then issued the order, which spelled out the higher commander's intent, priorities of work, and a time line for briefing the forward operations base commander about the order for infiltrating into the area. He began with a couple of important items of business. One, they needed a plan that made sense, and two, they needed supplies.

Not just any plan, but a straightforward one was in order. This was not going to be a complex mission. The men would follow the Ranger handbook's step-by-step "troop leading procedures" for planning a mission. All they had to do was follow the steps and they would be ready (at least that's what the Ranger handbook said).

Red and the captain divided the team roughly along the lines of a planning cell and a logistical cell. They needed to start formulating a plan that would begin with infiltration, describe actions on the objective, and then detail exfiltration and refit for follow-on missions. The logistics guys would have to get water, ammunition, weapons systems, barrier gear, and everything else the men were going to need to hold and fight for the valley for three days with the worst-case scenario in mind. They would not be walking into the valley, so it wasn't too big a deal to go in heavy. They could always destroy what they couldn't carry back to keep it out of the wrong hands.

Their commo (communications officer), T.T. Boy, worked with a battalion commo section to set up a broad communications plan. It was fairly complex, with a set of flow charts that described how they would communicate with the FOB, the AWACS, and the CJSOTF. The plan separated various forms of communications into four categories: primary, alternate, contingency, and emergency (PACE). The first three usually involved a radio of some type; the last, emergency, was stuff like signal mirrors, smoke, and running around naked. Emergency communications were important because if the whole world ended they would need a way to call for close air support, emergency resupply, or emergency exfil.

As for the various communications platforms, they had two satellite channels, VHF, UHF, FM, and HF radios. They also had interteam communications, a multiband interteam radio, and a PRC 5 for satellite communications (SATCOM). All of these had to be "filled" with a current encryption key to allow for secure communications. The radios were almost too secure, with technical problems if you so much as looked at them wrong. Each radio needed an antenna kit, wires, and batteries, lots and lots of batteries, which made for heavy loads to carry. With all his batteries, T.T. Boy ended up with a truly backbreaking rucksack, one of historic proportions in its weight-to-size ratio.

Meanwhile, Red got Stitch to analyze the intel summary of the area. He basically needed to know the entire history of

Deh Rawod and why they were doing what they were about to do. It turned out they had gathered quite a bit of intelligence on Deh Rawod through SIGINT, and from special recon teams sitting in the mountains around the town. These guys had been watching Deh Rawod for a few weeks, and there was an agreement that the area was in a defensive posture. There was a lot of antiaircraft artillery (AAA) firing at the sound of any aircraft in the area. That type of behavior was not typical and was based on some other intelligence that probably meant there were high-ranking Taliban personalities in the valley. The inhabitants of the Deh Rawod area were of the same ethnic group and clan as the Taliban leadership. Plus, Mullah Omar's extended family still lived in Deh Rawod, and it was his childhood home.

Ringo and Kev were given the job of gathering their logistical supplies. Red overheard the base commander telling the logistics guy that they had a blank check, that they were to get anything and everything they wanted. It wasn't as easy as it sounded. First Ringo and Kev would have to make a cohesive equipment requirements list. The time to scrounge up everything else was very limited—24 hours to plan and load for the mission. To make matters even more difficult, the men's bodies needed sleep.

Like they say, no rest for the weary, especially now when the race was on.

The forward operating base had a small conference room for planning. Rock and the captain worked on the tactical plan, while Red planned the necessary routes, including primary and secondary landing zones for infil and exfil. For this he used Falcon View, a software program that displays electronic maps of an entire country. All someone had to do was type in the coordinates of the location, and the corresponding map would appear. As you zoomed in, the map gave way to aerial photographs of the area. The resolution wasn't great. Ten-meter imagery was the best it could do, meaning you could see an object that was 10 square meters in size or larger on the photograph.

Red looked for a spot where they were going to set up the blocking position. He picked a helicopter landing zone close by. He chose an alternate blocking position site in case they couldn't land at the primary landing zone.

The plan was coming together. They would infil by a single MH-47 helicopter, a special operations variation of the Chinook. They would infil close to a support-by-fire position (adjacent to the landing zone) and unload the helicopter as quickly as possible. A Spectre AC-130 gunship would be readied so she could watch the surrounding landscape while they unloaded the MH-47. Then the men would move the barrier equipment by ATV to the road and set up a physical obstacle in the road that would prevent vehicles from passing them at any speed. Next, they would move to the support-by-fire position onto higher ground to cover the people at the blocking position. Then three of the men would move onto high ground to watch the valley for approaches.

They had an M240B machine gun capable of hitting targets a few thousand miles away, an SOF-specific Barrett .50-caliber sniper system, a 60mm mortar, and radios to call in fire support if necessary. They would maintain some of the supplies at the overwatch position (the concealed position where a sniper supports the advancing assault force by taking out the enemy).

They planned to go in heavy with an ATV, set up barriers for the blocking position, and set up support-by-fire and overwatch positions with crew-served weapons and sniper systems. They would be accompanied by five Afghan soldiers and an interpreter.

Noncombatants could come and go as they wished, but the bad guys were dead meat. For instance, if a truck or vehicles approached the blocking position and attempted to flee, the men would engage it, with Ringo's .50-caliber sniper system shooting the engines and drivers at range, and with mortar engaging units of any size trying to maneuver against them.

Red and the captain briefed the mission to the battalion commander the next day at the Task Force 160 tent next to the FOB. The briefing covered the night's air mission, the routes to the objective, the emergency plans to fall back on, the abort criteria, and the travel arrangements person by person. Two Spectre AC-130 gunships would clear out all threats forward of the route.

For the men of Beast 85, it was all about getting out into the field and silencing some al Qaeda and Taliban foes. They were pumped about the opportunity before them.

The battalion commander liked the concept, and at 1500 hours he gave Red and the captain the go-ahead.

The approved continuous operation (CONOP) plan looked like the following four pages on paper:

# BEAST 85'S MISSION CONOP*

CONOP FORMAT
(from Beast 85, to 60 FOB 32 for CJSOTF approval)

**SUBJECT:**          CONOP 85/003 (BEAST 85-03)
**REFERENCE:**        FRAGO 009 TO FOB 32 OPORD 02-001; MAP,
                      DEH RAWOD, 1:100,000, SHEET 2082, SERIES U611
**TIME ZONE:**        ZULU
**EXECUTING UNIT:**   BEAST 85

## TASK ORGANIZATION

| MSS/Overwatch Position **EAGLE** | Checkpoint Position **LION** | Support Position **FALCON** |
|---|---|---|
| 18Z Master Sergeant Red | 18B Staff Sergeant Frank | 18A Captain Alan |
| 18C Staff Sergeant John (SNIPER) | 18C Staff Sergeant Mike | 18E Staff Sergeant Tim |
| | 18C Staff Sergeant Kevin | 18B Staff Sergeant Mongo |
| 18C Staff Sergeant Joe (MORTAR) | 18F Sergeant First Class Steve | 18D Sergeant First Class Dave |
| USAF Terminal Air Controller | Personal Security Force | |
| | x 4 passengers | |
| | Interpreter | |

**SITUATION:** There were at least four separate incidents of AAA fire and possibly as many as seven separate incidents during the Norwegian special operations forces (NORSOF) SR infil between 101800zJun02 and 101905zJun02. The defensive posture is oriented around the city of Deh Rawod. The enemy likely mistook the SR infil for a direct-action mission targeting a person of perceived importance who was currently in Deh Rawod. Mullah Mohammed Omar's extended family reportedly lives in Deh Rawod and reporting from early June indicated that Berader may be in this area. The population of Deh Rawod is heavily supportive of the Taliban. Below are the reports of AAA fire and the reporting unit:

**AC-130 REPORTS INFORMATION AS FOLLOWS:**
101801zJun02     AAA 14.5mm
101825zJun02     AAA 14.5mm
101911zJun02     AAA 23mm+25PAX

---

*See the list of abbreviations in the back of the book for reference to acronyms used in CONOP plan.

**3/160TH PILOT REPORTS INFORMATION AS FOLLOWS:**
101820zJun02    AAA
101825zJun02    AAA
101828zJun02    AAA
101830zJun02    AAA
101900zJun02    AAA

## MISSION:
On order BEAST 85 conducts a rotary-wing infil into AO CARDINAL to establish a blocking position "Gibbs" NLT 132300zJun02, ivo grid 41, Valley Pass, to destroy enemy personnel and deny AQ and Taliban elements a safe haven within AO CARDINAL.

## EXECUTION:

**INTENT:** Beast 85 will accomplish this operation by conducting a rotary-wing infil into AO CARDINAL to establish blocking position "Gibbs." Decisive to this operation is our ability to effectively establish blocking position "Gibbs" prior to Beast 62 and 63 armed reconnaissance. This is decisive because it will allow Beast 85 to destroy AQ/Taliban forces attempting to depart the Deh Rawod location. End state for this operation is that enemy targets are destroyed and all Beast 85 personnel are safely returned to FOB 32 to refit and prepare for follow-on operations.

**KEY TASK:** Destroy al Qaeda/Taliban personnel/establish blocking position.

**CONCEPT OF THE OPERATION:** This operation will be conducted in six phases.

PHASE I ODA PLANNING (12–13 JUNE 2002)—DURING THIS PHASE, BEAST 85 WILL CONDUCT MISSION PLANNING INCLUDING:
    Develop and submit CONOP
    Receive CJSOTF approval
    Conduct parallel planning
    Issue FRAGO to detachment
    Give breifback to FOB 32 Commander

PHASE II INFIL (13 JUN 02)—DURING THIS PHASE, BEAST 85 WILL INFIL FROM KANDAHAR AF TO AO CARDINAL THE EVENING OF 13 JUNE VIA ROTARY-WING A/C.

PHASE III EXECUTION (14–16 JUN 02)—DURING THIS PHASE, BEAST 85 WILL CONDUCT BLOCKING POSITION INSTITUTIONAL OPERATOR TRAINING SHUT OFF THESE KEY LOCATIONS.

PHASE IV EXFIL (16–18 JUN 02)—DURING THIS PHASE, BEAST 85 WILL REDEPLOY VIA ROTARY-WING A/C.

PHASE V DEBRIEFING AND REFIT (17–18 JUN 02)—DURING THIS PHASE, BEAST 85 WILL CONDUCT DEBRIEFING AT KANDAHAR AIRFIELD.

**TASK TO MANEUVER UNITS:**

MSS/OVERWATCH:
 Conduct rotary-wing infil.
 Conduct linkup with interpreter and AMF.
 Establish an MSS and Overwatch suitable to support position
 and blocking element for three days.
 Maintain communications with AOB 24/7.
 Submit SITREPs NLT 1300z daily.
 Assist in blocking position duties.
 Conduct target interdiction of enemy targets.
 Call e-CAS.
 Call medevac.
 Receive QRF.
 Conduct rotary-wing exfil.

SUPPORT POSITION:
 Conduct rotary-wing infil.
 Conduct linkup with interpreter and AMF.
 Establish support position suitable to support block element for three days.
 Maintain communications with AOB 24/7.
 Submit SITREPs NLT 1300z daily.
 Assist in blocking position duties.
 Conduct target interdiction of enemy targets.
 Call e-CAS.
 Call medevac.
 Receive QRF.
 Conduct rotary-wing exfil.

MAIN EFFORT/BLOCKING POSITION:
 Conduct rotary-wing infil.
 Conduct linkup with interpreter and AMF.

Conduct interdiction of all suspected enemy personnel.

Submit SITREPs NLT 1200z daily.

Maintain an interdiction log.

Maintain communications with MSS 24/7.

Call e-CAS.

Call medevac.

Conduct rotary-wing exfil.

**TIMELINE:**

| | |
|---|---|
| 120930Z | STAFF MISSION IN BRIEF |
| 131230Z | AIR MISSION BRIEF |
| 121900Z | BRIEFBACK TO FOB COMMANDER |
| 122200Z | FIRE SUPPORT PLAN DUE |
| 131000Z | EPA DUE |
| 132200Z | NORSOF SR/64/85 EALT |
| 131630Z | BEAST 62/63 DEPART KANDAHAR AIRFIELD VIA MH47 |
| 131730Z | BEAST 85 INFIL PLZ BLADE / ALZ BLISTER |
| 132230Z | ESTABLISH BLOCKING POSITIONS |
| 16TBD | NORSOF/64/85 EXFIL |
| 17-18TBD | BEAST 62/63 RETURN TO BASE |

**INFIL:**

PRI LZ 41S BLADE

ALT LZ 41S BLISTER

**EXFIL:**

PRI LZ BLADE

ALT LZ 41S BLISTER

**RISK ASSESSMENT:** HIGH.

**RISKS:**

Contact en route to AO.

Contact at blocking positions.

Vehicle breakdown en route.

**MITIGATORS/ENABLERS:**

Rehearse and chalk-talk integrated air defense system prior to movement.

Maintain security during all phases of movement.

Maintain COMMO with FOB 32 24/7.

Platoon-size QRF can launch within 30 minutes of notification,
    a company in 60 minutes.

FOB 32 establish vehicle recovery plan.

**SERVICE AND SUPPORT:**

SERVICE: Deploy with six days of supply.

SUPPORT: No change.

The men began to pack straightaway. The amount of gear was staggering. Each man was going in with over a hundred pounds of ammunition and equipment. They figured on five gallons of water per man, 55 gallons per team per day. Over three days, that was more than 150 gallons of water. They had an ATV, wire, radios, batteries, ammo, crew-served guns, sniper systems, personal weapons, and a little food.

It was the first real combat mission that the team was to undertake. After being in country for a month, doing everything from sitting with their thumbs up their asses to filling sandbags for barriers and welding steel walls around AOB–North in Bagram, they had finally planned and were going to execute a real mission.

Red and the captain returned to the tent and went over final coordinating instructions. They briefed the rest of the team on the route in and out, the point of no return, and the abort criteria.

Red reviewed the final details of the plan and discovered, much to his surprise, that he would be carrying an M240B, a 28-pound crew-served machine gun, and 3,000 rounds of ammo. He didn't understand how or why this gun got assigned to him; this size of gun didn't seem to be the best choice for someone in his position. It was not that he minded carrying it, but he was a command-and-control guy.

Rock had planned the detailed actions at the blocking site, so Red asked him how this happened. He gave no good answer—nothing coherent, anyway. Screw it. Everyone was overloaded as it was, so assigning it to someone else was not an option. So he agreed to carry the fucking gun, along with 3,000 rounds of ammunition—about 60 pounds worth.

So this was it. Soon they would be "in the shit."

The light medium tactical vehicle (LMTV) was open, allowing Red to look out across the flat land surrounding the airfield. He wasn't scared, but more than a little apprehensive about the infil. It was like waiting for a race to start. The men were ready to run, but they had to get there first. As they drove to the far end of the runway where the TF-160 birds were staged, a few 101st Airborne Division guys looked up at them and figured out they were going to hunt al Qaeda and the Taliban. The team got the usual "hoo-ah" barks and battle cries.

Strangely, after all the waiting, it now felt to Red like they were going ahead before they were ready. They weren't particularly well rested, and they had zero time to rehearse. Other questions were racing through his head. What if they really weren't ready? What if the infil was a complete cluster fuck? What if the landing zone was hot (hostile), as expected? Dammit, he wanted to be on the ground. As long as they were in the air, there was nothing they could do but sit and wait for the impending chaos.

Upon reaching the airfield they linked up with five members of the Afghan Military Force, or "jundis" as they were known. The jundis were scared and had no idea what was going on, but there was no time for hand holding at this juncture. More to the point, there was no way Beast 85 was going to reveal any mission details to them prior to infil. Red simply told the jundis through the interpreter to get in the helicopter, to sit and stay put. The plan, once they landed, was to have these guys sit off to the side of the MH-47 while the rest of the men unloaded, then move them to the roadblock, where they would stop and search cars.

The MH-47 is discernable from its cousin by the huge refueling boom sticking out of its front. This bird flies at night, low to the ground, and is designed especially to get special operations teams in and out of the field. It has internal auxiliary fuel tanks providing 2,068 gallons of fuel, and it can refuel in flight if it runs low on gas.

The real magic of the MH-47 is the AN/AQQ-16 forward-looking infrared system (FLIR). Their bird's FLIR was projected on a large center-mounted video screen in the crew compartment. Hard to believe, but its integrated terrain-avoidance radar and computer let them fly the damn thing in the dark only a few feet above the sand dunes—quite a rush at 200 miles per hour.

But as tough and high-tech as their MH-47 was, it was still just a helicopter, and not all that hard to shoot down. They were going to be flying through a gauntlet of AAA sites to get to the infiltration site. They counted on speed and darkness to mask the bird's flight. Task Force 160 had been up the valley on several occasions and had experienced AAA every time. In the briefing, it was explained that the AAA sites were not radar guided, so the people shooting were aiming at sound rather than visual targets, and they kept missing.

Darkness began to fall as they finished loading their bird. Two helicopters away, the team destined for the blocking position to the north was also finishing up its preparations. C Company's sergeant major asked Red if there was anything they needed. He considered his options, thinking some German beer would be nice. Red told them that what they really needed he couldn't give them, which was more time to rehearse landing and unloading a thousand pounds of equipment.

Eleven operators, six jundis, one six-wheeled ATV over-loaded with barrier material and ammunition, and a huge war wagon of electronics that the special operations helicopter needed to work its night-flying magic. So after a manic four hours of planning, four hours of sleep, a briefback to the FOB commander, and six hours of frantically gathering ammo and supplies, here they were, packed like sardines in a black Chinook, ready as they would ever be.

The large internal fuel tanks divided the cargo compart-ment. Forward of the tanks were the crew doors, miniguns, and then the cockpit. There was a 2-foot-wide space on the right side of the tank for people to walk forward and aft of the tank. The remaining three-quarters made up the cargo compartment. Flipper and Red were all the way forward, on the far side of the fuel tank with the crew, door gunners, and the pilots. Behind them in the large cargo space was the ATV and the rest of the team. Red sat his machine gun and gym bag full of ammo down on the floor so his wouldn't break his back before he had to.

Once it was completely dark, the captain felt the heli-copter's engines change pitch, and they lifted off. As the big helicopter broke free of the ground, he felt a surge of excitement, and all the stress drained from his body. To this point his mind had raced wildly, bouncing from contingency to contingency, war-gaming courses of action, mental checklists, wondering if he missed anything.

They cleared Kandahar and headed into the mountains to the north. Next stop, Deh Rawod.

Under cover of darkness, they would be inserted approxi-mately 4 kilometers west of the Helmand River. After studying available imagery, the pilots determined the terrain there was too severe for a normal landing. So they would be doing a two-wheeled landing, in which the front two wheels of the big double-rotor-blade aircraft would remain hovering above the terrain while the rear wheels contacted the ground. It would look like they were popping a wheelie.

From this precarious position, the crew would lower the rear ramp, and the team would charge out into the darkness. Sounds exciting in a briefing, but in reality the potential for misalignment and ensuing disaster was high. If the terrain at the aircraft exit ascended severely enough, rotor-blade clearance from the ground would be minimal, and exiting operators could run into the deadly rotating blades. In other words, it could turn out to be a bloody mess.

But the captain didn't want to think about it right now. It was better to remain calm, so he let his eyes absorb the darkness that consumed the aircraft.

Hot air buffeted the cargo bay, and he watched the men's silhouettes shift in the darkness, trying to find a comfortable way to support the 100-plus pounds strapped to their bodies. It would be a 45-minute flight if all went well.

*Brrrrrrrrrrrrp.* Captain Alan was startled from his trance by the sound of the helicopter's miniguns being test-fired as they flew over the designated area. Two thousand rounds per minute spat from the weapon. The MH-47 has two miniguns on each side, next to the crew doors. They would be a formidable deterrent to anyone on the ground who decides to engage the gunship. They can suppress the enemy on the ground while in flight, or more importantly, while on the ground disgorging passengers onto a hot landing zone where the enemy is engaging them as they deplane.

The captain hadn't expected a test fire, and the noise sent his heart racing.

Kev sat in the 2-foot-long corridor created by the fuel tank. They all had on their night vision goggles (NVGs). The helicopter was totally black. Red had the advantage of being able either to look out of the door gunner's windows or to look at the FLIR display in the cockpit. He communicated with the crew by headset, and internally with the team by multiband interteam radio. The crew would provide him with time hacks, or readouts, which he would relay to the team, tracking each waypoint, or navigational landmark on the map.

Red was also responsible for giving 30-, 15-, 10-, 5-, 1-, and half-minute warnings as they progressed along their flight route. He estimated it would take 90 minutes. Once they landed, he would be the last guy off the bird, making sure no one forgot anything. Then the crew chief would signal the pilot to leave.

The helicopter was flying low and fast. The captain could hear the pilot talking to Spectre and to the helicopter bringing the other team. Spectre was flying forward of their route using its FLIR for forward recon, checking the terrain below their helicopters before they got to it. The fire-control systems were something to behold. From an altitude as high as 15,000 feet, the FLIR on Spectre could discern the type of weapon carried by an individual on the ground. The pilot could rain down 105mm, 40mm, or 20mm cannon fire on targets with stunning accuracy.

In other words, Spectre was one bad motherfucker. It was good to have it on their side.

Red motioned into the corridor at Kev to get his attention. It was hard to see in the dark cargo hold, even with the NVGs, and hard to hear from all the noise created by the two jet engines, which are loud enough to damage your ears without hearing protection. So he leaned around the corner, grabbed Kev by the shirt, and yelled into his ear, "Thirty minutes—pass it back!" He gave Red a thumbs-up and leaned over to the next dark shape in the cargo hold.

Then Red heard the door gunner shout, "AAA, port side!" Through night vision goggles, the enemy fire looked to the men like a serpentine of green blobs rushing upward. *Why the hell weren't the door gunners smoking the miniguns?* Red thought.

"They're shooting at the sound of the aircraft," reassured the crewman. They weren't engaging the helicopter, just shooting blindly skyward at the sound of the near-invisible aircraft. The fire was hundreds of meters off target.

The Spectre crew knew their business. To fire the miniguns would have rendered a visual clue to the gunman, and risk a more effective engagement from the ground. So the miniguns remained silent, and the MH-47 whizzed through it in a flash.

Then they turned east into the valley where they would be setting up the blocking position. The other helicopter continued north. Dipping and twisting, the experienced special operations pilot guided the aircraft with expertise as they raced toward their objective. Suddenly, in the midst of the blackness that filled the open ramp area of the helicopter, a green line serpentined skyward. Red relayed the 15-minute warning.

"What the hell was that?" Captain Alan yelled to nobody in particular.

Red heard again over the headset, "AAA port side!"

This meant it was no longer safe to cruise high above the hills and valleys. From now on, the pilots would fly nap-of-the-earth, racing up valleys at treetop level, diving down the back side of hills. This is the helicopter pilot's version of defensive driving; keeping the helicopter low to the ground would minimize the time that anyone on the ground had to engage it. By the time an aggressor had visual on the helicopter, it would already be out of sight.

They continued their flight toward the blocking position from the west, avoiding the town of Deh Rawod and racing east up the draw toward the Helmand River valley.

Suddenly, after flying over a totally desolate area, they spotted a collection of campfires and vehicles in the wilderness below, nowhere near any town. The crew member in the rear of the bird said the people around the fires were shooting at the helicopter—probably enemy fire. Business at the blocking position was going to be good.

"Ten minutes," Red called out.

At that point, the captain saw another streak of green blobs floating into the sky behind them. The remainder of the trip saw several more trails of tracer rounds serpentine harmlessly skyward to the rear of the aircraft. Through his headset, he could only make out only bits and pieces of the garbled conversation between the helicopter pilot and the orbiting AC-130 Spectre gunship whose job it was to cover their infiltration with deadly accurate fire from 15,000 feet above the ground.

*Five minutes.* Red leaned around to Kev, yelling for him to pass back the word: Get ready.

*Two minutes.* The helicopter ducked over a ridgeline as it sped toward the landing zone. Instantly, it was spotlighted from a large light source on the hillside behind. The beam shone into the back of the blacked-out aircraft and followed the helicopter as it contoured down the slope. The muzzle flashes in the darkness confirmed that they were being engaged from the hillside by small-arms fire. Like a prizefighter ducking under a punch, the aircraft dropped sharply below the ridgeline and followed the rutted draws down the mountain toward the river valley.

Behind them Captain Alan lost view of the ground as a brownout of dust and dirt engulfed the helicopter.

*One minute.* Red could feel the bird slow down. The crew had been given the exact coordinates of the primary landing zone. As the helicopter approached, the pilot hovered in search of a place to land. The terrain was much worse than the Falcon View 10-meter imagery had given it credit for. It was not remotely as flat as was indicated; on the contrary, the slope of the hill was about 45 degrees, with boulders scattered all over it.

They continued to hover, slipping left and right, pushing up a huge amount of dust. Finally, the pilot announced that he was heading to the alternate landing zone, farther east, near the mouth of the draw and the Helmand. Red said fine, and passed the word back.

There was some concern about a mountain to the right of their flight path. Intel had shown them a large 22.7mm AAA site on that same mountain. It was unlikely they could lower the gun far enough to shoot down into the draw, but it made the men nervous.

With their eye on the mountain, they tried to land at the alternate landing zone, but had similar results. The terrain was too steep. Red told the pilot to find a landing zone of opportunity and land. They could adjust the plan if they had to, but it was better to get on the ground before those assholes around the campfires showed up. The bird whirled and hummed, slipping sideways down the hill toward the floor of the draw. Red looked out the window on the port side. The terrain was pretty treacherous. The helicopter hovered for a second and started down.

*Thirty seconds.* Everyone on the aircraft was poised to rush the ramp as soon as the crew member gave them the thumbs-up. The captain flicked on his electronic aim-point sighting device and prepared to flip in an instant from "safe" to "semiautomatic." His index finger ran along the top of the trigger well of his M4, and he held the collapsible butt-stock deep into his shoulder pocket.

One last deep breath, a forcible exhale, and they were ready to go. Captain Alan felt the weight on his legs increase exponentially as the pilot flared the helicopter in preparation for touchdown.

Those closest to the rear stood on the ramp waiting to jump out. About 25 feet from landing, the rotor wash began to form a massive cloud of dust, totally obscuring the ground. The pilot accelerated toward the ground in an attempt to stick the MH-47 on terra firma.

Suddenly, with the groaning noise of metal being torn apart, followed by a huge bang, they were thrown into chaos. Two crew members at the ramp looked a little frantic.

Shit, something was wrong, and they hadn't even landed yet.

Red got the attention of a crew member and asked him if there was a problem. The crew member looked him square in the face. "A problem?" he huffed. "Fuck yes, we have a problem!"

By now their headsets were alive with aircrew chatter as the pilots tried to assess the situation.

"Abort, abort, abort," came the call across the headset, and the helicopter pitched forward and staggered down the mountain draw toward the valley floor.

A tremendous shock sent the captain crashing to the floor of the aircraft, knocking the wind out of him. Red, too, was thrown to the ground, and Flipper, with his 100-pound rucksack, landed on top of him. The engines screamed, and their senses told them that the aircraft was rolling over, listing to the port side. They could see rings of sparks flying from the rotor blades, which were tilted toward the ground, chewing up thick clumps of dirt and dust.

The smell of ozone filled the cargo space. The men's eyes burned with the dust and their nostrils filled with the acrid smell of burning hydraulic fluid. They struggled to get to their feet, and their minds reeled as they tried to orient themselves to the situation. Were they shot? Just as it seemed they would topple over and roll down the hillside, they felt the aircraft lurch upward and sway side to side.

A fraction of a second later, the helicopter jumped up in the air about 25 feet and hovered. To say that was the hardest landing (or rather, landing *attempt*) any of them had ever experienced would be putting it mildly.

Recalling the fate of Navy SEAL Neil Roberts during Operation Anaconda, Red and Captain Alan struggled to get a head count. There had been five team members aft of the captain's position, and there were five silhouettes staggering to their feet.

Red figured their pilot would give it another shot, but then he noticed the crew was turning on white lights and rushing around looking at control displays. His headset had stopped working, so he couldn't hear a damn word. He glanced behind him, toward the ramp. Again, smoke and sparks, all in NVG green, bellowed into the cargo compartment from the port side of the ramp.

Despite the overwhelming urge to shut up and let the pilot get them the hell out of there, the captain shouted, "Can we insert onto our alternate landing zone?" The calmness in his voice as he asked the question took great effort.

"Negative!"

The pilot's response sounded final, but Captain Alan persisted. "Just put us in on the flats of the river banks, and we will hoof it from there."

Red grabbed a crew member and yelled above the engine noise, "Are we going to infil or not?"

"Negative, we have been ordered to return to the airbase, the infil is aborted."

That was it. They would not be inserted.

The next thing the captain knew, someone began thrusting containers into his hands. "Pass it back!" He recognized the container—hydraulic fluid. That couldn't be good. "Here!" Another can came, then another, and another. For the entire 45-minute return flight the men shuffled cans of the critical fluid to the back of the aircraft where a crew member poured it into the leaking system. One guy was flat on his stomach, examining the helicopter's underside.

They continued east in their crippled bird into the Helmand River valley, then turned south toward Deh Rawod. Red looked out the gunner's window as the valley opened up below. Despite what they had just been through, and what lay ahead, he couldn't help noticing how beautiful it was. The valley was miles wide. The river looked large, and there were crops growing on both sides. As they flew over Deh Rawod, another row of tracers arched up in the air behind them. It was as if they were bidding farewell. Red felt like flipping them off in response.

Then by some miracle, his headset started to work again. He asked the pilot what had happened. The pilot told him the bird had crashed onto something that had torn the hydraulics out of the bottom. They had been able to isolate the problem, and he expected the helicopter to make it back to Kandahar.

On the way back to Kandahar, the men received word that the NORSOF team had run out of water and was critically short of supplies, so they headed to their special recon site to conduct an aerial resupply. The NORSOF team was perched high up on a mountain overlooking Deh Rawod. A large gathering of ground crew was there to greet them. The helicopter hardly moved for the 20 minutes it spent hovered over a sheer drop of several thousand feet with the rear ramp touching the top of the mountain and the nose sticking out into space. The team passed the supplies out the back to the NORSOF guys, who were happy to receive the emergency resupply.

As soon as the supplies were unloaded, the men went back to the task of shuttling can after can of hydraulic fluid while the pilots skillfully nursed the broken aircraft home. An hour later, they flew into Kandahar Airfield. As a member of the ground crew brought a jack-stand to bear under the tail of the aircraft, the helicopter came to rest, and the engines decelerated. The men piled off the aircraft, and got their first good view of the damaged Chinook. The right rear wheel had been broken off and jammed up into the tail section of the aircraft. A large chunk of the tail was missing, and the skin of the ramp had been torn off. Fluid, presumably the precious hydraulic fluid that they had poured into the aircraft during the flight back, pooled on the tarmac.

Captain Alan told Red that another MH-47 was warming up with the intention to infil a NORSOF team into the area.

But their team's mission was the top priority. With only a few hours of darkness left, it made sense to bump the NORSOF infil for another infil attempt of their own in the new Chinook. The captain requested and received permission from the forward base to attempt another infil, and Red talked to the Norwegian recon team commander, who agreed that his team's blocking position could wait another night.

The members of TF 160, however, were not on board with the idea. The Night Stalkers, as they are called, refused to refly the mission. To them, it wasn't worth the risk. No way. Not with large groups of people up the valley anticipating the next infil attempt, not with the length of time the team would spend in the draw.

Maybe they were right, but that didn't make the news any easier to accept as the team spent another two hours unloading the helicopter and waiting for a ride back to the tents. Ringo rode the ATV back to the compound, grabbed an LMTV, and drove back to pick up the rest of the team. They went back to the compound, and back to bed.

It was a final dead end. The night was over. You wouldn't know it from the faces of the team members, which were euphoric with the adrenaline high of the heavy action and the near miss. Everyone was animated and speaking at a frantic pace about what had happened and who had seen what, when, and why. Pictures were taken, stories swapped.

Kev caught Ringo on videotape acting out a fantastical skit in which he contemplated launching himself and the four-wheeler full of barrier materials and ammunition out the back of the damaged helicopter before it left the crash site. Loud, comical, and surreal in the greenish light of the low-level camera, it was a rare glimpse of Ringo getting caught up in the emotions of a situation and losing his customary cool. They all felt the same thing.

So there they were, on a dark runway lined with undiscovered land mines, a broken helicopter sitting motionless next to them. No one came from the FOB to pick them up. No one came to get accountability of a team that had encountered enemy fire during infiltration, crash-landed, recovered, and limped home. They had everybody from the team safely back at the airfield, but no one seemed to care. It had been an unbelievable night, and just like that, it was over.

• • •

The mission they hoped would net a thousand al Qaeda and Taliban forces netted nothing. Not a damn thing. The team that infiltrated to the north ended up next to a village and spent two days hiding from the villagers. The two teams that were pushing up from the north were late by almost a day. Someone had picked up what was thought to be one of Mullah Omar's bodyguard's cell phones in the valley that night, but in the end, no one acted on the intel.

Red stood in the operations center listening to the lieutenant colonel tell one of the teams on the ground to move a few hundred meters north, or south, whatever. Instead of leaving it up to the guys on the ground to decide, they had made a habit of using a bad map, one almost universally agreed to be lacking in accuracy, to maneuver the teams. It was more about control than getting it right.

But new plans were being drawn up even before Beast 85's mission was declared over. Soon they would be attaching to C Company along with their sister team, Beast 83. There was going to be a big follow-on mission to occupy a firebase back in Deh Rawod, home of the Taliban, but first there would be a large combined arms mission up the valley—Operation Full Throttle. Full Throttle was going to be a major combat operation, meant to stick a finger in the eye of the Deh Rawod area's Taliban support network.

Three special recon teams had been in the mountains around the town to collect intel showing persons of interest still in the area. The FOB wanted a toehold in the area so they could push farther north into the central mountains. They were convinced that Deh Rawod was hiding hoards of bad guys. Forces would enter the town and search the entire place, denying the enemy sanctuary. So after a week of sitting around Kandahar Airfield, the men were given a warning order: plan for Full Throttle.

Beast 83 was released from its administrative job and reassigned to the mission. Beasts 85 and 83 would make up one of the assault troops, Beast 12 and Beast 13 would make up the other. Early in the mission planning it was going to divide the objectives roughly into two parts. First they would air-assault into positions and roll to their objectives. Battalions of the Royal Marines and the 101st Airborne Division were going to air assault into the valley and seal the town.

Once the town was sealed, they could work their objectives and let the 101st do a broad and comprehensive search of the entire town. Studying the maps, Red thought two battalions weren't going to cut it. Three battalions would have been more like it.

The new assault unit began planning the hit. They were given a fairly large stretch of real estate along the western side of the Helmand River, north of Deh Rawod, and just along the Shart'oghay Mountains, called "Named Area of Interest 32-107" (NAI 32-107), or Objective Green. They positively identified a number of mud compounds, and gave them snake species for code names, such as Viper and Asp. Objective Green was thought to be where Mullah Barader (the number two–ranking Taliban) resided, and within its boundaries were a 23mm AAA gun, an unknown number of enemy soldiers, and a complex of bunkers and caves. They identified more than 15 full compounds for their objective, essentially the entire village of Shart'oghay.

This was too much for a single 24-man element to take on. They needed to whittle it down. Red and Captain Alan approached the intel officer and asked him to select the compound he thought was the highest-value target. He had no idea which of the compounds was of more value. Red asked if there were any national intelligence assets (CIA) who could help pinpoint the exact compound Mullah Barader might have lived in at some point. The officer said he would look into it, but he never did get back to him.

Without much help from the intel puke (their affectionate term for the guys in military intelligence, particularly those who never have the right intel when you need it), the men coordinated limits and split the targets with Beast 83, and after briefing the roiling assault plan to the FOB, it was approved.

But before they knew what hit them, things changed. The approved plan suddenly disappeared. By 27 June, the air assault was called off. Instead, they were told they would drive 60 vehicles from Kandahar to the objective, planning to "surprise" the Taliban.

Yeah, right.

The way it usually worked with special forces teams was to give them a desired "end state," and leave it to the men to decide how to best achieve it. Now, the higher-ups were again micromanaging the course of action. There was no arguing. They were told that this was simply how it was going to be, period. End of story.

Even worse, the men of the assault unit found out that the battalion of Royal Marines, the 82nd, and the 101st would not be joining them as was hoped. Instead, the men would drive up and set up a blocking force around Objective Green. That way, Afghan army guys with their 19th "group handlers" could land a helicopter and search upwards of 30 compounds themselves.

"Oh my God," Red thought. With this kind of plan, they weren't going to be sneaking up on anyone. A novice war planner could see that this was nonsense. The mission was not going to work, and both teams knew it. Morale plummeted.

It didn't matter to the FOB commander. He was hell-bent to see it through, full of prophecies of routing the enemy. The assault element was going to have an impressive amount of airpower joining the combined forces of Beast 85, Beast 83, the Company B-team, a platoon of Navy SEALs, a few guys from the CIA, and about 30 vehicles. But all the guys knew that with such a scheme, any fuck-up was going to have very real consequences. And there was a very real chance for a fuck-up.

# CHAPTER 8

# THE VALLEY OF THE CHILDREN

*Beast 85 left Kandahar for its assault on Taliban positions more than a hundred kilometers away to begin Operation Full Throttle, 14 June 2002.*

The assault unit moved from the badlands through the tiny town of Pïtaw. From there, they moved up the first foothills of the awesome Spin Ghar mountain range, which lined the dimming horizon 6 kilometers to their north. They drove up and over a distinct-looking hill (also called Pïtaw), which made for an easy landmark to pick up on their map. It was a fantastic hill stacked with the rocks, debris, and rubble that had washed like dirt out of the mountain range. Along the trail to the top of the hill they came upon a graveyard.

To Red, Afghan graveyards were especially spooky. Afghanis have an interesting way of treating their dead, burying them in the ground where they fall. It's common to see stone graves set 1 foot off a road, or on the side of a hill in the middle of nowhere. Strips of cloth hang from long, gangly branches of wood among the random rock stacks scattered through the graveyard. These places reminded him of the movie *The Blair Witch Project*.

It gave him pause to consider how the various beaten souls came to be buried in these barren, isolated places.

Their convoy made its way down the north side of the hill, stopping partway to rig for blackout drive. The men tested their night vision devices and mounted them on their helmets. The vehicles had infrared lights to illuminate the way for people with night vision goggles, but they remained invisible to those without night vision. Unfortunately, if the bad guys had night vision, the assault teams were screwed. Their vehicles would be visible for miles.

It wasn't enough to merely turn off the lights; bumping the switch back to "on" would have spelled disaster. They couldn't chance it. So Ringo rigged both sides of their truck by pulling the light bulbs out of the back lenses as well as both the turn signal and headlight fuses.

They started at noon hoping that six hours of daylight would be enough time to get them through the Spin Ghar Mountain pass. An hour-plus delay waiting for the SEALs fucked up the schedule. It meant that for the rest of the trip they would have no visible light. They would be driving on night vision, in the pitch black looking through NVGs. This was not exactly ideal, considering the tricky terrain. The changes in depth perception always made night vision driving especially difficult.

When you're wearing NVGs, the whole world takes on a green hue. The darker the object, the deeper the green. By burning up the terrain ahead with two infrared lights, distinctions in hue were virtually impossible to judge. Basically, everything was light green. Problem was, if you drifted off the road and weren't aware of it, particularly in a mountainous region, you could be royally screwed.

Red walked back along the convoy to discuss the remaining route to the mission support site with Major R., particularly the winding trail to the Spin Ghar Mountains that followed east to an ominous-sounding mountain pass known as the Valley of the Children.

The two men exchanged small talk about the route already traveled, then decided it was best to stay on blackout drive for as long as they could safely get away with it. If the mountain terrain was too dangerous to continue driving on night vision, they would radio the lead vehicle to go to white light. Only the lead could turn on lights, because bright lights could potentially blind someone wearing NVGs. Once they rigged for white-light drive, they could go off night vision.

Red joined the rest of the guys from the team, who were at the lead vehicle dining on MREs and talking shit, waiting for total darkness. He grabbed a bite himself, enjoying a luxurious canteen of hot water with his dinner. They still had a long way to go.

Once night fell they were ready to start the next leg of the trip. They weren't even down the hill when they ran into their first snafu. Turning on their NVGs, they found that the trail was even less distinct than they expected. The contrast on the ground, easily discernable by day, was lost under infrared light at night.

Red wanted to take the road that would link them with the main route north through the Valley of the Children. The trails were getting crisscrossed and confusing, but they were able to see a trail that headed left. They trusted their map and turned, with 30 vehicles behind them.

The trail took them straight to the driveway of a compound. They pushed back, turned around, and tried to pick their way around the compound, struggling to make their way east. One road—or rather, dried riverbed—they found looked promising, so off they went with their convoy to the rear. Then they came to a wall of rock and debris. It was a dead end.

They decided to backtrack and try a second option, a road heading north toward the mountains. As their vehicle moved back through the convoy, a difficult situation became that much more chaotic when dust clouds turned the whole world green.

Major R. wasn't exactly the epitome of calm as the captain relayed instructions to him while Red concentrated on coordinating GPR with the map and the terrain outside, using only a small finger light. While the truck bounced over miles of rutted roads, his navigation developed a sort of rhythm, "NVGs on, look around, NVGs off, finger light on, look at the map, look at the GPR," over and over. And they still had miles to go to their objective.

It soon became obvious that the new road was the main road, and their only real option. Thankfully, it was much deeper into the mountainside than it appeared on the maps. This was good from a navigational standpoint. On flat ground, roads simply disappeared in the green of the NVGs, but a road like this one, cut out of the rock, is clear and much easier to follow.

So the men were back on track, heading toward the Valley of the Children. The land became increasingly steep as they drove east, then north. The road was rutted with rocks and dirt, but the path remained clear. Then they moved into the Spin Ghar Mountains. Red looked at the map, and the Valley of the Children was the only point through the mountains for miles. The convoy would be in the ideal position for an enemy ambush.

The Valley of the Children followed a trickling stream and was 15 kilometers long. The road had been blasted through the rock and cut through the mountains. It was like driving through the Grand Canyon, only on a smaller scale.

The assault element crawled, curved, and swept along the road at the bottom of the gorge like a snake. The men surveyed the scene around them; no moon, no natural light, and the scope of the terrain was enormous. In the darkness that enveloped them, the mountains appeared through night vision as thousand-foot walls of green rock, fading into dark green shadows, and the sky over the valley as a mass of irregular black shapes. The gorge spread 2 miles at its widest. A sense of danger was ever-present.

They could hardly be farther from any possible help. Air support bombing, the great equalizer in this war, would never be able to get to them. The gorge would be too narrow and deep for an aircraft to drop ordnance. The enemy would be on a higher part of the terrain, so if they were bombed, the enemy, along with the mountain, would fall down on top of the convoy. With no threat of being bombed, they could hit the trail and lead vehicles, then destroy the rest of the convoy at their leisure. To make matters worse, the assault was not exactly approaching in stealth; their had been no stealth to speak of since Kandahar.

The dangers of the terrain made it even more difficult. The risk of accident grew greater by the minute. It became clear that the men needed white light. So it was decided that Red would signal the convoy when they approached the village of Daylanÿr where the pass opened up into a larger valley. Then they would go back to blackout drive.

At least they were on the right road. They crept along at about five miles per hour, crossing the stream over and over as they wound their way up and down the pass through the mountains. Ringo was setting a steady pace, and Captain Alan relayed information back to them on the status of the rest of the convoy. It was around 2200 hours, and they were getting tired. Rock and Doc Ken were in the back of the truck watching the sights through their NVGs. Red reminded them to look for bad guys.

Red took what must have been his tenth dip of chewing tobacco for the day. Ringo took a dip too, but Rock and Doc Ken declined. One of the few bonuses of going into combat is that tobacco just doesn't seem as dangerous as it does back home. Red considered dipping instant coffee as well to stay awake, or popping Ripped Fuel (which contained ephedrine for energy).

With his dip in place, Red passed word to the captain that they were approaching the end of the valley. There was a truck stop of sorts, which must have been running on a generator. The lead vehicle cut its lights and crept forward to take a look while the rest of the convoy waited. There were two white buildings on the left side of the road and another smaller one on the right. Outside there were a few "jingle trucks," the highly ornate Afghan cargo trucks, and a small group of men sitting outside drinking tea. No sign of crew-served weapons, no fighting positions, no heavily armed people. All clear.

They rolled through the truck stop slowly, looking around for potential trouble. The people drinking tea smiled and waved—middle-aged tribesmen with the requisite beards, bottle-cap hats, and turbans, the local garb of choice. Red guessed the truck stop doubled as a bus stop, and the tea-drinkers were drivers enjoying the cool of the night. He waved back, with no illusions that these men were as friendly as they appeared. He expected their movements would soon be broadcast (the low-tech way, via rapid word of mouth) to bad guys all over southern Afghanistan.

Red radioed the captain that the coast was clear, and the rest of the convoy started moving behind them. Just outside the mouth of the valley was the village of Daylanÿr. Daylanÿr and the valley beyond it surrounded by mountains were flat, dusty, and dark.

Suddenly, they found themselves clear of the pass. Good timing, because nature was calling most of the men. After a piss break, they went back to blackout drive. They drove past the dark village of Daylanÿr for about half a kilometer and pulled over. Red's head was aching, his back hurting, his muscles and nerve-endings buzzing from energy pills, dip, and no food.

The air was very dry. The assault element was at a position about 10,000 feet above sea level, with no city lights for hundreds of miles. They were well into the night, and still had a long way to go. Red rechecked his route and talked small talk with the guys about the amazing night they were witnessing. Without the moon, the stars washed across the sky with an unusual intensity.

From there they moved northwest for about 20 more kilometers before nearing the mission support site (MSS). They turned left past Daylanÿr and west toward the final leg of the trip. As they entered the plains, the road smudged into the brown of the land. It was impossible to tell through NVGs if they were even on a road. Red compared the map to the surrounding terrain to try to find out where the hell they were. The road continued to appear and then disappear, fading into the night vision background, as the convoy crept from waypoint to waypoint.

The vehicles in back continued to deal with a huge dust cloud from the trucks and humvees in front. Red felt bad for them, but at the same time, glad to be out in front of the dust as it rolled over the plains. Doc Ken drove as they started to drift away from the waypoint again. Red asked him to see if he could get them back on track by picking his way to the right.

They started moving south toward what they hoped was a route that would align them with the row of points on the GPR screen. Red noticed what looked like a wadi (dry riverbed) in the way. They were driving right into it. He told Doc Ken, "Dude, I wouldn't drive through that wadi." Meanwhile, Ringo was sleeping in the back, missing all the action.

Before they knew it, *boom!*, they were nose down in the damn thing with their rear wheels sticking up in the air. Captain Alan was behind them in his GMV. He jumped out. The men shook off the cobwebs that had collected on their brains from all the sleep deprivation, tied a cable around the Toyota's bumper, and yanked it out of the ditch with the GMV. Then the men jumped back in their vehicles and pushed west in the green darkness as if nothing had happened.

More excitement was in store for the last part of the trip. Twice, the entire convoy had to backtrack to find a way through to what might have been the main road. At the time, Red, Ringo, Doc Ken, and Rock were not picking up a lot of airwave chatter. That was probably for the better. It meant they were blissfully unaware of Major R.'s laments and howls. His concern: by not reaching the MSS prior to sunrise, they were going to lose their "stealth."

*Stealth?* My god, he must have been living on another planet.

Fourteen hours into the trip they approached the village of Sardāgh. The road ended at a compound's front gate. People were sleeping outside on wood-framed beds with rope mattresses.

After a short search, they found another road leading south toward the Spin Ghar Mountains and the village of Gumbad Kalay over Tōr Ghar Hill. The assault element followed it over the hill to find a riverbed winding to the west. The trail into the riverbed was damn steep. Red wasn't sure the truck could make it down, so he walked it first. He decided it was worth the risk. The rest of the convoy followed their truck down the hill into the darkness ahead. Red hoped like hell they weren't heading to another dead end. They wouldn't have time to backtrack an entire convoy again and make their objective.

They drove for another 500 meters or so until they boxed in the compound. To their right was the trail they wanted. They turned and headed west, with Red breathing a sigh of relief. The one-lane trail wound through the village. Walled orchards closed in on them as they bumped up a hill, past the village, and up toward rockier ground. The terrain cleared up but then became rocky west of Sardagh.

It was 0430 hours when they broke out of the plain and back into the foothills near the MSS. The terrain was still tough and rocky and getting steeper. Fatigued to the core, Red fell into a trance for a while, which the captain broke to tell him teams from Tarin Kowt had beckoned them with an infrared strobe, meaning they knew they might be approaching. The strobe, invisible to the naked eye, is easily seen through night vision. Red called for everyone to take a good look around.

Then suddenly, off to the left about half a kilometer, Red saw it—a blinking light. It was the strobe. Suddenly he knew how Columbus must have felt. But after driving nonstop for 17 hours, they hadn't exactly crossed an ocean. They had, in fact, only covered about 150 kilometers.

# CHAPTER 9

# OPERATION FULL THROTTLE

*The men of the assault element turned their thoughts to the other side of the globe. As Beast 85 sifted through Afghanistan, hunting al Qaeda and Taliban, rescue workers in New York City sifted through the ruins of 9/11. Both searches were marked by a combination of frustration and determination:*

*    **7 May:** Rescue workers reported that no human remains other than small bones had been found in weeks.*

*    **28 May:** The last standing steel beam had been cut down and removed.*

*    **30 May:** Rescue workers and victims' relatives held a ceremony to mark the end of remains recovery.*

*    **2 June:** Families gathered at the site for a remembrance ceremony.*

The convoy drove toward the strobe as a new day started with a pink sky. A small secondary trail took them up a question mark–shaped valley with rounded hills on all sides. They turned into the draw where a group of U.S. soldiers in desert camouflage were waiting, ready to assign their sectors of responsibility in the MSS. Beast 85's position would be in the center of the draw.

They pulled in and aligned their trucks and humvees four abreast, while the other teams charged up the hills surrounding their little valley to set up their newly assigned sectors of security. Silhouetted against the skyline, the Navy SEALs went to the crest of the hill. They were then told to bring their vehicles down the slope in defilade. They seemed a little out of their element. Needless to say, this was a long way from the sea.

The hills surrounding them were several hundred feet high and had about a 50-degree grade. They were covered with small brown rocks of all shapes, like everything else in the valley. Two teams from the firebase in Tarin Kowt had also made the trip to the MSS. Together they made up the entire assault force.

The men piled out of their vehicles and started to lament the 17-hour ride up from Kandahar. They were tired, dirty, and hungry. The dust from the road was almost white. It frosted their hair and added about 40 years to their faces. It was a better aging effect than any Hollywood makeup artist could create.

The teams would break into assault configurations prior to leaving the MSS, but for the moment they were to stick together as one. Red confirmed the priorities of work with Drinkwine: prep vehicles, cover them up, study the contingency plans for if they were attacked, eat, sleep. They were expecting a plan from the assault element's leadership that they were to study. For some reason, it never came.

The team covered the windshields and other major reflective surfaces of the vehicles with camouflage netting, gassed up all the vehicles, made sure the major weapons systems worked and were loaded, devised a quick detachment plan, set up some shade between the trucks, and went to sleep.

Direct sunlight was still behind the hills, but once the sun rose, the temperature would skyrocket to well above 100 degrees Fahrenheit. Red laid down in the dirt, between the trucks under a tarp, waved his arms and legs like a snow angel to push the rocks out of the way, and went into a deep sleep on the spot.

He slept for about three-and-a-half hours. It was a dreamless, deep sleep, the kind of sleep your body needs during an abbreviated sleep cycle. When you push a sleep-deprived body, it starts to make due on 15 minutes here, an hour or two there, 30 minutes there. If you get the sleep, even in that fashion, your body can go for days. But without a lot of sleep, the mind loses its cognitive ability, and you begin to hallucinate. You can't think clearly. Strange, then, that the first thing that gets planned away in military operations is sleep.

Often in the military things are done a certain way because they've always been done a certain way, not because there is a logical reason. Logic is secondary. It should not be surprising, then, that Beast 85 was asked to make a long, harrowing overland movement when there were helicopters sitting on the tarmac at Bagram Airbase, collecting dust.

• • •

Red awoke as if from a coma, from a black, dark, dreamless place. The oppressive heat and terrible noise of someone choking to death pulled him out of the depths of his sleep. He looked to his left under the truck and saw a sleeping medic, Doc Hoss, on the other side, surrounded by other members of the team. True to form, Doc Hoss lay on his stomach, snoring in his nasty, loud, gagging way (he was a renowned snoring machine), his arms stretched straight behind him, a river of drool running out of his mouth and down his sleeping mat to his leg.

For half a second after Red awoke, he felt like a helpless infant, without a clue as to where he was or what was going on. He knew nothing and understood less. At the same moment, he inhaled a breath of the oppressively hot air that felt like it was sucking the life out of him.

Doc's snoring shocked Red back to his difficult reality. He was disgusted and fascinated, unable to look away. You could even say he was mesmerized, in a very strange way. He's not a mean person by nature, but his first instinct was to throw rocks at the medic to get him to stop. Maybe part of it was just plain boredom. Anyway, Red hit him with one rock on top of his head a little harder that he anticipated.

Doc Hoss stopped mid-snore, but did not wake up. Then his sleeping brain seemed to process what was going on. He warmed up to snore again, so Red threw another stone, this time with greater care. It hit Doc lightly on the neck. He stopped snoring.

Red's interests soon turned away from toying with Doc and toward getting out of the heat. He needed water. He needed food. He needed a fresh dip of tobacco. He needed Ripped Fuel.

He also needed to finalize the assault plan and schedule a final precombat brief, get coordinating instructions, and talk to the 3rd SFGA teams about the route to the objective—25 objectives, in reality. The last 17 hours of driving did little to convince him that they could find their way across the Helmand River and up to Big Top, the first objective.

Not really. The first objective was water. If you don't drink plenty of water, you will perish in this environment. So Red walked to his Toyota and slid one of the 5-gallon water jugs free of the straps that held it to the back of the truck. He poured the water into his hand and drank it, savoring the plastic taste of 120-degree liquid refreshment. He would repeat this ritual more than 10 times a day to try to keep his body hydrated.

You can check your hydration by the color of your urine. Clear urine means you're hydrated, and the deeper the yellow, the greater the dehydration. Red's urine, and everyone else's, was consistently dark yellow.

Red then walked toward 83's area in the middle of the draw. Two of their humvees were up on the northern hill. They were around the agency guys and the B-team guys from Beast 60. It was getting really hot.

While "Jake," a guy from the special tactics squadron, cleaned his rifle, Red chitchatted with Rock about the previous night's movement and how fucked up it was. Drinkwine set a time line for teams to coordinate plans, orders of movement, travel modes, and destinations. The only change that Red knew of was that he was going to end up driving the armored humvee along with Captain Alan, Jake, and "Wishbone" from Beast 83 in the command vehicle. Otherwise, the teams were going to remain intact.

As the B-team coordinated their own major moving parts, Red stopped by to check out their plan. Sergeant Major "Trails," a tall, lanky guy with a cadaverous face, was milling around Beast 60's area. Red greeted him and asked when the final coordination meeting would be, assuming that a meeting was planned. Trails didn't know but would pass the word when he found out. He then complimented Red on his job leading the convoy the night before.

As Red walked away, the B-team's operations sergeant, "Sam North," popped out from behind a car. He liked Sam. He was smart, personable, and realistic. But Sam was the one who picked the route from Kandahar Airfield to the MSS based on faulty maps and imagery of the area. Red walked up and shook his hand. "Nice fucking route," he said.

He laughed and made a remark that the route was fine; it was the person doing the navigating that fucked things up. Red told him he would see him at the meeting, but that for now he must run. He had to talk to the guys from Beast 62 about the route to Big Top. He would find them in a group of vehicles on top of the southern hill.

The earth in this part of Afghanistan is covered by a collection of rocks ranging in size from large pebbles to as big as your head. Many of the rocks looked like they came from different places. They had different colors and textures and were scattered with a consistent density over everything. The dirt between the rocks was so dry that it became a finely powdered dust if disturbed.

As Red walked up the southern hill, he searched for a cool rock for a souvenir. The rocks themselves seemed to be melting into the dust. The tops of the rocks were cracked and lined; the centers appeared normal for rocks, but the bottoms were covered with a hard white coating, and the texture looked like they were being consumed by the hill itself. He found the rock he wanted to keep just as he trudged to the top of the hill.

The guys from Beast 62 were hanging around their vehicles. Red walked up to the same guy who had guided them into the MSS earlier that morning. No one wore their rank insignia, so you couldn't tell who was who. He spotted the guy he wanted to talk to, a noncom, an older-looking guy, sitting on his ass against a GMV. Red asked if he could help with the route they were going to take to Objective Big Top on the western side of the river. "Sure can," he said.

Red opened the map and tried to show him their positions along the route to their objective. His fingertip was too large to point with precision, so he looked for a pointer, a stick, something with a small tip. He looked around on the ground. Nothing. *This damn desolate landscape*, he thought. It was the first time in his life he couldn't find so much as a twig to use as a pointer.

He fumbled around in his map case and finally found a suitable tool, a mechanical pencil. He showed the older guy their route, down into the Helmand River valley, up toward Deh Rawod, to the release point where they would go west toward the river, and the rest of the element would move toward Deh Rawod. From the release point, Red traced the route down toward the river. The big question was where they were going to cross the river. They would be approaching the river at night using 1:100,000-scale maps. He needed to know the precise location of the ford site to cross the Helmand.

They would also be relying on information from Beast 60. A few weeks ago, there had been extensive reconnaissance of the ford site. A major wadi, the Karnale Mandeh Wadi, ran down into the river from the east. The ford site was where the wadi met the river.

Once across the river, they were going to pick up a trail that followed the western shore to the north. They would cross the river and simply turn right, following the river trail straight to their first objective. Red traced the route on the map. Once they crossed the river, the route would be clear and fast. It was the only trail north, and they couldn't miss it, even at night using

NVGs. Other teams had driven past the same position over the previous few weeks without problem.

So Red took a dip of tobacco and headed to the bottom of the hill. The captain was sitting on the hood of his GMV snacking. Most of the team was awake. It was getting way too hot to sleep. Red told the captain what he had been up to. He was interested in the route because Beast 85 was going to be leading the entire convoy. He showed the captain the route on the map, including the Karnale Mandeh Wadi.

The captain agreed that the route was solid. They had the assurance of a team that had driven the route only a week prior. One of them, Jake from the special tactics squadron, had been on a recon mission in the mountains surrounding the objective about a month before and informed them that it was a 30-mile-per-hour road. Maybe things would work out. Red hoped so. In general, though, he thought the plan sucked. A good route was not going to change a bad plan.

Red found Drinkwine and told him he could discuss the route to the primary ford site with the teams whenever they were ready.

Time passed slowly. Lying in the dirt, Red thought about the strange sequence of events that had led him to this place. There he was in a small valley waiting for the big push into the Helmand River valley to look for the bad guys. Last time he had been there was three weeks earlier during the now-infamous helicopter ride.

The sky was a perfect light blue, clear for as far as the eye could see. It was a day like every other. Red walked back to the 83 area. Drinkwine was there. Red told him he could brief the route to their teams in 30 minutes if Drinkwine wanted. He agreed, and the word was put out to the teams.

As everyone sat around the large map of the area, Red went over the order of march. Beast 85 would lead, with the captain in front. Connor, Jake, Drinkwine, and Red would follow in their humvee as the command and control element, and Beast 83 would come up behind them. Their assault element would lead the convoy, and the other 24-odd vehicles would follow.

There were a few questions about the rules of engagement. Red told them to kill anyone who posed a threat—no one was going to second-guess an individual's decision to use deadly force. Captain Alan went over the actions on the objective. Rock and his team would lock down Big Top as they set up the landing zone to bring the helicopters with the 19th SFGA teams onto the objective, then Teams 83 and 85 would move to blocking positions north and south of the objective as the Afghan army soldiers with their 19th SFGA handlers moved through the compounds. After the support-by-fire positions were confirmed, everyone knew what they were supposed to do.

Red had the guys prep the vehicles, check the radios and weapons systems, and rest. It was getting to be a late afternoon, and Beast 60 had just called for their meeting to put out final coordination instructions.

All the element leaders sat around Beast 60 team's cluster of vehicles as Major R. had his staff briefed on the final instructions and went over the very complicated air-support plan and a few other things. For the air plan, timing was the key. Close air support would be waiting for the go-ahead if they needed it.

The last item was about the checkpoint. The route into the Helmand River valley went through a mountain pass. Toward the end of the pass was an Afghan military checkpoint run by the governor of Uruzgan province, Jan Mohammed. They wanted to stop the checkpoint from tipping their hand to the local authorities as they crept into the valley with 30 vehicles. If they did so, the bad guys would either run away or lie in wait for an ambush. The idea was to take the checkpoint's radios and satellite phones, preventing them from making the call after they passed the checkpoint.

Question: How would they prevent the guard from making the call as he watched them approach the checkpoint at 5 miles per hour? Answer: They would have to take down the guard post. But Sergeant Major Trails didn't want them to use deadly force. He emphasized this to the teams. Red begged to differ. That decision was firmly in the hands of the Afghans at the guard post. They could cooperate or they could die.

The briefing lasted an hour; it was about two hours from kickoff.

An hour later, Red moved into the humvee with Drinkwine, Jake, and Wishbone up top. He would drive so that Jake could communicate with the air-support element, Wishbone could smoke bad guys with the MK19, and the captain could command the assault element. Red cursed Rock for putting him in this job during mission planning, and cursed himself for not turning it down. He got his radio out, checked the configurations, and did a communications check. It worked fine.

By now he had pretty much memorized the route. The humvee, for all of its size, had very cramped seats. He got his shit organized and tried to make his temporary home as comfortable as possible. He was going to be in that vehicle for hours and hours. Red smirked, glad it was the captain this time, not him, who would have to endure the misery of leading the pack.

They were to be on the objective by midnight, so hopefully the route would be clear. Seven hours were all they had to move 25 kilometers to the objective across impossible terrain. They would be cutting it close, so everything had to be perfect. If one cog in the machine was out of synch, they were all screwed.

They rolled out of the MSS site at first darkness, 1745 hours. Red thought to himself, "Here we go. This is what I've been training to do for all these years." He wondered how many people sitting in their mud homes right that second would be dead when the sun came up. Did they have any premonition that the grim reaper was coming to take them?

While he was concerned about someone on his team getting killed, he didn't really think about his own death. But to him, nothing in this damned wasteland was worth losing one of his guys over.

The road north ended at the Deh Rawod to Tarin Kowt west-east road. They went west toward the Anarak Ghar Mountains. The route was through a pass and then down to the Helmand River valley. Beast 62 reported that the road was so steep in places that the brake fluid in the humvees would boil if they braked too often. They would have to rely largely on the transmission to slow the vehicle.

The road west quickly started to climb up into the Anarak Ghar Mountains as the sun crept behind the mountains.

Red soon discovered that his communications radio, which had worked when he tested it, would only work when he stuck the antenna out of the gun turret above his head or out the window. The armor in the humvee was killing the radio's signal.

Using night vision, Red steered along the rutted trail behind one of the Toyotas. Kev was behind the M240B, Bubble Boy was driving. Red watched Kev try to take the jolting of the truck over the stones with his legs. He knew all the gunners in the back of trucks were getting rattled pretty hard by the ride.

After traveling for about an hour, the lead vehicle spotted the Afghan army outpost on the downhill slope to the Helmand River valley. They stopped about 200 meters short of the outpost. Men from Beast 83 dismounted their vehicles and moved toward a small structure sitting on the mountainside to Red's right. It was about 100 meters up a path from the road. Bubble Boy was moving to Red's left with his sniper gun, looking for a position from which he could observe the target through his night vision scope and kill anyone approaching it while the assault team went in. Red told Wishbone to stand by with his MK19. He felt the turret swing the MK19 toward the shack. He waited. Then, he saw Sergeant Major Trails walking toward the guard shack. "What is he up to?" Red wondered.

He started becoming impatient. Time was wasting. The entire assault force was pressing on his back waiting to push past this holdup and get on with the mission.

Thirty minutes later, people started getting back into their vehicles, and Captain Alan radioed that they were rolling. Red later learned that Sergeant Major Trails, in the interest of being "nice," talked the Afghani in the guard shack out of his radio. Red couldn't believe he wouldn't just take it from him. The guard was no fool and agreed to hand everything over.

Oh, and another thing. The guard had mentioned getting a call one hour earlier telling him that a 30-vehicle American convoy was en route to his checkpoint, arriving in about an hour.

Their cover had been blown the moment they left Kandahar Airfield!

The checkpoint was on the Helmand side of the pass. They were on the downhill run to the broad valley that spread out below. They headed for the release point where they would break off to the river while the rest of the assault force could continue north toward Deh Rawod. Red looked to the rear of his vehicle. Beast 85 and 83 were on blackout drive. The rest of the convoy was on white light. A snake of vehicle lights mixed with clouds of dust wound its way down the pass and into the valley. It would be visible for miles and miles. Red got on the radio and screamed for everyone to go to blackout drive. No response. He knew the major's truck was somewhere in the middle of the convoy. He yelled over the radio again to go to blackout drive.

At that second, a stream of heavy machine-gun fire raced up into the sky from the valley floor. The tracers, representing every fifth round, looked huge, puffy, and green in night vision. They left the ground at about a 45-degree angle and waved up to about 60 degrees in the three or four seconds of the burst. There was no sound. The bad guys had been waiting for them. No one had wanted to turn off their lights for Red a second before, but they started to go off in a hurry after that.

Back on blackout drive, they drove farther down into the valley toward the heavy machine-gun fire. Kev was up and on the gun in front. They continued on toward the release point. The landscape on the valley floor opened up. The terrain wasn't as flat as the maps suggested. The road followed along ridge tops, into and out of washes, and onto more ridges, roughly aligning with the river below.

Red's vehicle broke off and headed toward the river, promptly followed by a group of Navy SEAL vehicles, with the rest of the convoy continuing north. Red stopped the vehicle to have a word with the SEALs. It turned out that the navy guys were with the wrong group, and their eyes widened when they realized that they had broken contact with their element. The captain tried to give them directions back up the hill so they could rejoin their group. They departed in a rush.

Red started up again, steering the vehicle down toward the river. Another line of tracer fire aimed into the sky erupted to their front. As he watched the truck in front of him, he saw that Kev saw it, too, and he physically responded to the sight by moving into the gun mounted on the back of the truck. The road toward the river ended in a T-intersection at the village of Cekzai. They turned right to follow the river north toward the major draw the 3rd Group team pointed out as their ford site.

They picked their way north, and eventually found a wadi they had been looking for. The Karnale Mandeh Wadi made a major cut through the hilly landscape, and there was a road that followed within it toward the river, which was about 500 meters to their left. They moved into the wadi. It was about 50 meters wide and opened up as it washed into the river. Along the sides were 10-meter-high cliffs. The terrain favored the Taliban, so they moved the element toward the river hoping to find the ford site quickly.

The vehicles to their front stopped at the river. Red saw a couple of stunted trees, a few ruined walls, and some dim lights—what looked to be the village of Dizak.

Jake was listening to the air control network as the aircraft started to check in. The first-wave aircraft were starting to circle a few miles away, waiting for the order to move over the objective area.

Two AC-130 Spectre gunships checked in. Two B-52 bombers checked in. A few fighter jets checked in. Red hoped for better visuals. Things were running late, their radios weren't working, and they were tired after the 15-hour ride upvalley.

They rushed onward to the planned preassault fires. The special recon teams were going to call in AAA sites for Spectre to destroy prior to the assault teams moving to their initial assault points. Red was increasingly concerned that they would be late if they didn't get across the river and up the road. He figured the captain and the rest of Beast 85 were looking for the ford site.

Red got out of the vehicle. He needed to find out what was going on with the ford. Beast 85's vehicles were out in front along the wash. Behind him were the rest of the vehicles channeled in the narrow wadi. He walked down toward the river.

The moonless night was dark as pitch. Red saw Mongo and asked him what was going on. He told him the wadi ran into a 6-foot-wide irrigation ditch. They couldn't even get down to the river from the wadi. And Beast 62 had told them to go down this very wadi. Their GPR put them exactly where they needed to be. Beast 62 couldn't have driven the route, or they would have known about the irrigation ditch. Red returned to the command vehicle and told Drinkwine that they would have to find a way around the irrigation ditch, otherwise, they would have to go back the way they came, head north, and try to find the alternate ford site.

Red looked north along the riverbank when he saw a dark figure quickly approaching the convoy. He moved forward, looking at the figure through his night vision. He could make out the top half of his body. He was either running toward them or was on a bike riding toward them. Red lifted his rifle, acquired the target with his aim-point, set his selector switch to single shot, and placed his finger on the trigger. He waited for the figure to present more of his front, and then he would take his shot.

Behind and above him Wishbone, who was on the MK19 in the humvee, yelled, "Run, Red! *Run!*"

From his vantage, it looked to Red like the figure had some friends following him. His pulse was really pounding now. He flipped his selector switch back to safe and ran back to the vehicle, turned and scanned for the hordes he knew were running down the river path toward them. Then he saw one figure close to the captain's vehicles. The figure turned, and Red was nearly blinded by the infrared light on his helmet shining brightly through his NVGs. It was one of their own guys. It was unnerving for Red to think how close he was to pulling the trigger.

Things were getting a little out of control. On cue, two dark vehicles roared up to the cliffs behind them, looking down into the wadi. Red collected himself, spun around, and lifted up his rifle. He heard Wishbone turning the torrent of the MK19 around. Two black vehicles were driving without lights. They stopped for a second and turned around and left. The men found out later they were part of a lost SEAL platoon that was driving around looking for the rest of their guys.

It was time to leave. First, Red spoke to Drinkwine briefly. He was trying to make the radios work, but without any luck. Jake piped in that the air support packages had all checked in and were coming on station. Spectre was in the house.

A heavy machine gun opened fire from the far bank of the river over their heads. The tracers were big. It was probably 22.7mm AAA cannon fire. This time the rounds were not being fired harmlessly into the air, but directly at them from across the river. Red ducked, and slapped Jake on the leg. He shouted for him to call in air support on the position. Jake grabbed his radio, but before he could say a word Drinkwine told him to stand by, to wait. He didn't want to tip their hand to the enemy, who quite possibly didn't know where they were, and therefore, didn't know where to aim.

Arguing with the bastard would have done Red no good, but if it had been his call he would have directed that ordnance be dropped on that position. They were supposed to have inbound helicopters flying up the valley in a few hours, sitting ducks for that gun.

*Fuck it*, Red thought. They were too exposed. It was time to leave the wadi.

Captain Alan was unable to find a way around the irrigation ditch, so they headed south to see if there was another road turning down to the river. They agreed and started rolling. The vehicles all turned around and left the way they came in, right out of the Karnale Mandeh Wadi and continued south. They called their situation into the FOB over the SATCOM link on the sergeant major's radio.

The men picked their way in their vehicles through the village of Cekzai. In the darkness the mud walls of the village rose up on both sides of the road. Red could see people sleeping on the roofs of the buildings in the walled compounds. Suddenly the entire world lit up around them as if someone had turned on a huge spotlight. The light was only visible with NVGs. Red's blood froze. He snapped his head skyward as the convoy stopped. There was a point of light in the sky. It was Spectre, lighting them up with an infrared spotlight. *Holy shit!*

Red yelled at Jake to mark their position with their own infrared strobe, to get on the fucking radio to that aircraft and make sure they knew they were aiming at friendly forces.

The captain heard over the command net a very excited Puerto Rican voice yelling, "Beast eight five, beast eight five, you've got to stop, another unit is going to fire you up!"

That unit was the lost and marauding Navy SEAL platoon. They were way too far north of their area, they saw Beast 85, figured they were bad guys, and called in close air support on their convoy.

Red's strobe was on and out the window in a second. Jake was talking to the AWACs. They had received the call for fire and were looking around for another convoy because they had their eye on Beast 85's position for some time, marked as friendly. They had not been as close to pulling the trigger as Red had thought.

The eye in the sky turned off, and Spectre disappeared into the blackness of night.

It seemed like they would never find another trail down to the river, so they decided to head to the alternate ford site. They would return to the point where they had first taken the right at the T-intersection.

Just east of the T-intersection the convoy stopped. Red, Rock, Drinkwine, and the captain got out of the vehicles, took out the map, and plotted a route to the alternate ford site. They agreed that the captain would send two trucks to recon the route and return to this location to pick up the rest of the convoy. The original timeline was scrapped.

The two trucks sped into the night, turning right at the T-intersection and heading north, past the wadi they just left, looking for a primary trail to the alternate site about 4 kilometers north.

Red chomped down a Ripped Fuel, grabbed a dip, and talked to Rock about how things were turning out. Little did they know that the FOB was getting ready to write Red and Captain Alan's team out of the plan.

Meanwhile, they were exactly where Beast 62 told them to be when, *bam!*, they came upon a 6-foot-wide irrigation ditch.

It became clear to Red, Captain Alan, and the others in that instant that no one from Beast 62 had ever actually been there. Their claim that they had crossed the river at that point had been a lie, and a goddamn dangerous one at that. They had been bullshitted about the ford site, and were floundering because of it.

The two trucks reappeared about 40 minutes later. They had found the way north. The assault team got back in their vehicles and sped north looking for the alternate ford site.

They were climbing a set of hills and were heading down to the river when the lead vehicles stopped suddenly. The captain passed the word back that they were approaching the river again. But they had taken some gunfire from a small set of mud compounds that lined the river bank, so the captain asked permission to attack the compounds.

Because Red didn't have a working radio, he didn't know whether their attempts to move to the alternate ford site had been relayed back to the forward base by the 3rd Group's sergeant major and the company's second-in-command, who were following their convoy. They were now within 200 meters of the alternate ford site when they were ordered to stop, circle the wagons, and get ready to react to on-call missions as a quick reaction force.

So the trip to the Big Top was called off. With typical 20/20 hindsight, the forward base later told them that if they had known how close they were to the river they would have given them permission to continue to try to get across.

The assaults to the north were about to go down, so friendly fire was still a real danger. The captain moved his lead vehicles back, and they set up a loose area perimeter around the ridge-line. The word went out that one man in three could sleep, that they were to watch their sectors, and that they should stand by ready to move.

Red sat in the humvee, listening to Jake's radio. Suddenly it came alive as the assault started to form. Helicopters moved up the valley, and enemy AAA sites up and down the Helmand started to open fire—23mm antiaircraft fire, and 12.7mm dushka machine gun rounds, the now-familiar big green blobs streaming upward through the night vision goggles—taking aim at the sounds of the helicopters and the aircraft flying overhead.

The special recon teams called in Spectre on the AAA sites. The attack lasted almost two hours. Big Top was shot to pieces by a combination of B-52 bombers dropping JDAMs and Spectre fire. Next, Spectre targeted the compound on the border of the village from which AAA and small arms had been fired.

The result was devastating. Adjacent to the AAA site was a compound filled with partygoers celebrating a wedding. Spectre had fired its weapons into the adjacent compound, killing scores of civilians.

Once the scope of the friendly fire incident was known by headquarters, the assault was stopped. Medics from 19th Group made calls for choppers to evacuate the civilians. The task force commander in Bagram was awakened and informed. He quickly authorized U.S. military medical facilities to be used to treat the wounded civilians. A stream of CH-47s flew up and down the valley that night evacuating the wounded. There was no trace of the Taliban.

A word about the air crews: The aircraft were flying over a combat area, and they were receiving heavy antiaircraft fire from various ground targets arrayed in a gauntlet of antiaircraft artillery. There was an investigation, and the gun tapes were reviewed. Hindsight always blurs the fact that in the moment of the fight, people have to make decisions with limited information. They had to make a decision quickly, and the consequences of this decision were disastrous. Sadly, if they had to do it again, it would have happened the same way. It doesn't take away from the tragedy, nor does it take away the anguish felt by the survivors.

• • •

By the time Beast 85 returned to base, world media was already spinning, calling the operation the "Wedding Party Massacre" in response to Afghan claims that the skyward gunfire was simply wedding celebratory gunfire. President Karzai condemned the operation as a horrible mistake and demanded an investigation. Rumors about civilian casualties skyrocketed, claiming as many as one thousand civilians were killed. The Bush administration immediately stepped into damage control mode. Much to the dismay of those involved in the operation, none of their leaders disputed the inaccuracies reported in the press.

Those on the ground and in the air knew the difference between celebratory rounds fired randomly and shilka antiaircraft fire. There was no mistaking a couple of shots from a shoulder-fired kalashnikov and a 14.7mm dushka heavy machine gun being leveled at you from across a river. But the truth was lost in the whirlwind of finger-pointing and defensive posturing.

It was the first such operation for Captain Alan, Red, and the rest of the team. The experience changed forever what they understood about the reality and brutality of war. More importantly, it irreversibly changed the way the joint task force in Bagram would prosecute, or more accurately, avoid prosecuting the war.

. . .

The assault teams from 3rd SFGA had attacked the wrong compound. The 19th SFGA teams with their Afghan troops were dropped off at the landing zone to guard the compound after the attack. Rather than conducting additional searches of suspected compounds, as was the original plan, they handcuffed civilians instead.

Later, one of the 19th group guys told Red that he noticed radio antennas on the roofs of the compound just as they were about to attack it. As they began to maneuver toward the compound with the Afghan forces, they were stopped by the 3rd SFGA teams, which were sitting outside the wrong compound and were told to hold fast. They were not to move toward their objective. At the time, no one told them why.

There were heated exchanges over the radio. Once the extent of civilian casualties became known, all operations were ordered stopped by the forward operations base. Teams started to provide care to the wounded civilians. Red heard the medevac request from a 19th Group medic asking for helicopters to evacuate the wounded children so they wouldn't die from their wounds. As he listened, he didn't hear a single word about the capture of high-value targets.

Red called for instructions.

"Beast eight five, you stay right there," came back the order.

"How long?" he asked.

"24 hours."

At the time, Red suspected something significant had happened, and worried that they would become the focus of a lot of anger down the road.

# CHAPTER 10

# ON THEIR OWN

By early evening they reached Kandahar. There were no after-action review invitations. A plan that had called for a battalion of light infantry sealing off the entire town, followed by a detailed house-by-house search, had turned into a two-day drive to non-existent ford sites and mass aerial destruction. Nine weeks of duty in Afghanistan, and all Beast 85 had witnessed was inaction, incompetence, and now the massacre of 54 innocent victims.

The day after returning to Kandahar, they were told to move back to Deh Rawod and set up a firebase there. The plan was to drive to Tarin Kowt, the provincial capital of Uruzgan, link up with another 3rd Group team, then move to Deh Rawod. Beast 83 would set up in Tarin Kowt with the Charlie Company B-team and another team from 3rd Group.

Bravo Company, Beast 85's company, would be taking over the mission in the Helmand River valley area, replacing Charlie Company, which currently had a few teams spread over the Pakistani border and two teams in Ozgon district. The B-team was going to move to Tarin Kowt. Bravo Company was going to be OPCON to Charlie Company, and was to move up in a little while.

Major B. was not pleased. He wanted his company kept together in the field.

Bravo Company rented three jingle trucks—old Bedford trucks decorated with small bells and colorful paint—from a local truck company. By 8 July, the men had loaded everything they owned into the local trucks for the move to Tarin Kowt and then onto Deh Rawod. Red was surprised they couldn't get military transportation to move their gear, but like the hundreds of helicopters that sat on the runways of Kandahar Airfield, they were simply "not available."

The men of Bravo Company waited next to their trucks for two days. Then on the tenth, they were told to move out to Tarin Kowt. They requested dedicated air cover to support the movement, but were denied.

The trip took 11 hours and followed the exact same route that Red, the captain, and the others had taken a few weeks earlier up to the Valley of the Children. They passed through that same valley and then headed north instead of turning west.

Bravo Company met their escort at midnight and arrived in the compound in Tarin Kowt at 0100. Then their six combat vehicles and two packed jingle trucks moved into the compound. They parked away from the walls, then the men sprawled out and went to sleep.

The firebase in Tarin Kowt was a newly annexed building, rented from the governor, Jan Mohammed. Old Jan was not considered trustworthy, and was known to play both sides against the middle. He was all about personal power and fortune. He knew where the Taliban was hiding, but that was because he was being paid to hide them. He was part of the same tribe as the two Taliban leaders, Mullah Omar and Mullah Osmani.

The firebase itself was in the town and was surrounded by a 20-foot wall. There was a central structure built of brick and adobe, a mosque, and a few out buildings. There was no plumbing and no electricity. There were buildings up high so people could easily attack the inside of the place, throw a grenade over the wall, or drive a car bomb next to it. It was a rotten location, and it was going to be impossible to protect in case of attack. Red hated the place from the start.

The B-team from Charlie Company and some support guys were already in the compound. They had a security force of ethnic Hazaras. There were about 15 guys with AK-47s. Two 3rd Group teams were living in a large building behind the governor's palace about two miles away, and these guys had a reputation of sitting on their asses. This was the same crew that had lied to Red's face about the ford site during Operation Full Throttle. He went over to see them and confirmed that they would be ready to go the next day (as much as you can confirm something with a bunch of bullshitters). Red returned to the firebase.

Red was sitting and talking with the Charlie Company commander when they heard a distant explosion, followed by visible smoke. They rolled out of the compound in two vehicles toward the sound and the smoke, which led them to the police station.

The station buildings looked like a construction site where the work was never quite finished. The side building was billowing smoke, the window glass had been completely blown out, and smoldering bedding was lying in the yard in front of the side building.

An interpreter told them that two young guys had been messing with a rocket-propelled grenade inside one of the rooms when it went off. It had detonated into the floor at their feet. Flesh and blood were splattered all over the room, but no bodies—

at least, no intact bodies that Red could see. Then a police chief explained that the pair of men had managed to survive and were now on a bus to Kandahar. In his opinion, they were not going to survive much longer, not with those horrific injuries.

Red had a hard time sleeping that night. The buildings stored heat during the day and bled it off at night, so it was hot inside his cramped room for hours after sundown. He might have considered sleeping outside along with the other guys, but he preferred the protection of the walls. He tried to encourage them to do the same, or at least sleep behind the short wall in front of the building. It would be too easy for someone to lob a hand grenade at their vulnerable position.

But they didn't listen. Then at about 0400 hours, Red awoke to a loud thump. He was still in a fog of semiconsciousness when the next thump went off right outside the door of his room. The bright flash that accompanied the noise had him up in a blink. He searched for his M4 in the darkness then ran out the door. Dirt was falling out of the sky. He crouched next to the low wall. The clattering of automatic fire came from his right. He could hear rounds hitting the compound wall.

*Fuck me*, he thought.

Red crouched and stepped back into the room. The captain was already up. Kev came and told them what they already knew—that they were under attack. Red told Kev to get his body armor on, grab his gun, and wait for him at the low wall. Then he put on his own body armor and helmet, grabbed a pistol, threw on flip-flops, and moved to the low wall.

The automatic fire continued, but he was unsure about the tactical situation. It sounded like the firing was coming from the right. Spidey, who had been injured, called to Red to have a look at him. He had a long, bloody gash along his left eye and down his face. The wound was scary but not life-threatening. Red told Spidey to watch the front and shoot anyone attempting to climb the wall. Spidey collected himself and manned the position.

The men of Beast 83 were also up on their feet, barking orders and acknowledgments. Red stepped out from the wall and ran around the corner of a building where three of their vehicles were parked, and where four of the team had been sleeping.

Ringo and Rock were up and moving in the direction of the firing. They moved around the mosque to see if anyone was trying to breach the walls. Red ordered Flipper and Bubble Boy to head to the roof with machine guns, and to fire back at the motherfuckers who were shooting at them.

Rock, Ringo, and Red moved around the mosque to the wall. There were wooden guard posts in each corner of the compound. A Hazara militia was manning the guard post in the direction of the firing, shooting like a madman. The Taliban kept shooting at him, and Red kept shooting back with the tenacity of an entire militia squad. The firing went on for a couple more minutes, then subsided.

Everyone poked their heads out of the doors and windows. Red told Stitch to get one of their armored vehicles and an MK19, and told the guys to gear up, to get ready to roll. They were going to hunt down the assholes who were firing at them.

But before they could get under way Red was called to the company commander's room. Beast 83's team sergeant, Rock, its commander, and the captain were there with Major S. He was expecting marching orders, expecting to regain the momentum, to fire and maneuver, shock, unnerve, and give relentless chase to the enemy, as they were trained to do. He was expecting to advance and strike, advance and strike, until the assailant either surrendered or died.

In that spirit, Red started off by saying, "Sir, Beast eight five is ready to roll, sir. All men and equipment ready, sir."

The sergeant major's reply would echo in his mind long after: "Not so fast, not so fast."

Red knew what he meant. They weren't going to do a damn thing. They were going to let the bad guys get away.

The sergeant major was worried about formalities. He would send an emergency CONOP for permission from the forward operations base and the CJSOTF to leave the firebase and hunt down the Taliban. It would be scanned for grammatical errors, and staff clerks would check it for clarity (e.g., "Did you mean 'attack' or 'ambush?' 'Pursuit' or 'effort?'")

By now, there was no hope of capturing their attackers. Someone from Beast 83 asked if Red and the others should wait for the signal, then race around town in a show of force. It sounded to Red like a joke, but to Major S., it sounded like a good idea.

Some joke.

Major S. even called the forward base to see if they could find an aircraft in the area to do a fly-over. Meanwhile, Red and the others sat on their asses for almost two hours before getting their eagerly awaited permission to drive around the block and "show force."

The enemy learned an important lesson that night. They could attack the firebase and get away with it. Red wondered how long it would be before they would launch another, more daring attack.

The men learned important lessons about their leadership that night, lessons that were not so easy to swallow. War, especially in Afghanistan, is filled with uncertainty, risk, and chance. But amid this uncertainty, a golden opportunity fell into their laps and they had not acted upon it. The FOB had blocked their tactical decision. The insistence on micromanaging curtailed their true combat power.

• • •

Unlike the men from Beast 85, the FOB staff was not made up of citizen-soldiers but regular army. Both the army's noncommissioned and commissioned officer corps work on an up-or-out system. As soon as an officer spends a year or so in a job and really learns it, he is moved out of that job to follow his career path. While this is necessary in order to have senior officers who understand the spectrum of jobs under them, it also causes a lack of expertise and a reluctance to assume risks. In the National Guard, things aren't quite as bad because officers stay at the same rank longer and there is less job movement. In the army, though, upward focus means decisions are being made to please higher commanders rather than make the most operational sense. Turns out, if you think special forces are adaptive and decentralized, you're wrong. Special forces are in the hands of career-minded officers, to be demoralized and squandered.

CHAPTER **11**

# WHAT ARE WE HERE FOR?

*A 1916 order from the German Oberste Heeresleitung (High Command) reads: "It is strictly forbidden to delay local counterattacks while permission of the next higher headquarters is requested." Beast 85 saw this rule applied to ridiculous extremes: "It is strictly forbidden to go after the enemy until CONOP has been properly sent and acknowledged, wording has been checked and corrected, FOB has sought permission from CJSOTF and obtained such permission, and, and, and. . . ."*

Tarin Kowt was an ill-located, ill-protected firebase, led by a career-minded commander who displayed neither initiative nor daring nor resolve—three qualities most experts consider essential to waging a special forces war.

Fortunately, Tarin Kowt was a mere stopover for the men of Beast 85. They loaded their vehicles and happily left the fort behind on 13 July to move to Deh Rawod with Beast 63, the 3rd Group team.

They drove west toward the Anarak Ghar Mountains, as they had during Full Throttle. This time they climbed up and over the pass in daylight. After passing through the mountains, they came out onto the Helmand River valley and turned north toward Deh Rawod. Then they passed the attempted ford site on the hilltop and continued north. They moved east along the outskirts of Deh Rawod, which ran west-east along the Rûd-e Teri tributary.

At a spot on the border where the village ends abruptly and the landscape turns dry and barren, unable to support any life, they found their firebase. The front door faced south to the mountains and the desert. Behind them stood the fertile green zone and the village and fields of Deh Rawod.

The firebase was divided roughly into two compounds with a central wall between the two. There were mazes of smaller compounds in the back with lots of zigzagging walls. Beast 85 moved into the main compound. On the right side of the compound was a modern building, at least by the architectural standards of Deh Rawod. It was concrete, with marble floors, wired for electricity, and had overhead fans. In the front there was a fountain.

The left part of the compound was set farther back. It was a single-story adobe structure with six rooms. As the men approached it, they found it unbearably hot. Beast 63 had already staked their claim to the more modern right side, leaving Beast 85 the left side.

Their side might have been smaller, but their courtyard was bigger. They could line up their vehicles, and there was room for all the guys to sleep. A long, narrow covered front porch provided shelter from the day's heat. Red and the captain split the two small single rooms on either side of the building, with the other guys bunking up in the larger rooms. It was not much, but it was going to be home for the rest of their deployment. There was a

This Deh Rawod store exemplifies the local economy, which was very poor. The only crops they grew were opium and marijuana.

Red's room in Deh Rawod was hot and made of mud.

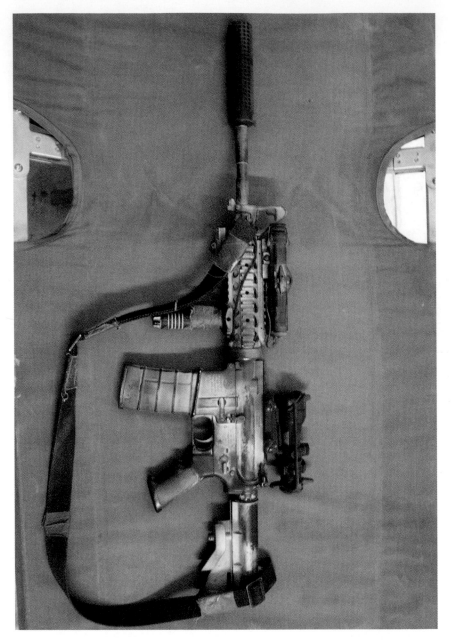

Red had a world-class weapon system in his M4, a simply great gun.
The bad guys didn't have anything that came close to it. Here it's fitted
with the SOPMOD kit, an invisible laser used with night vision, a
suppressor, and an X4 ACOG.

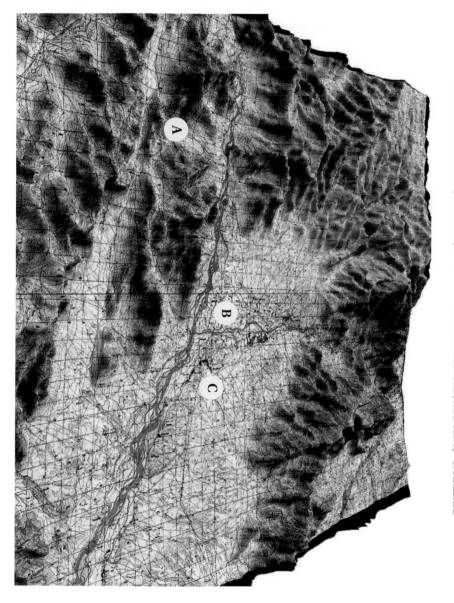

TOPOLOGICAL MAP OF DEH RAWOD REGION

**A:** HELICOPTER CRASH (CHAPTER 7) • **B:** WEDDING PARTY MASSACRE (CHAPTER 9) • **C:** FIREBASE

Doc Hoss at Firebase Gecko.

The whiteboard at Firebase Geckos' OPCEN illustrates Beast 85's sense of humor in making fun of themselves.

Beast 85, Firebase Gecko, August 2002. From left to right: Kev, the captain, T.T. Boy, Bubble Boy, Spidey, Red, Rock (all the way in the back), Stitch (kneeling), Doc Hoss (behind Stitch), Flipper (on the machine gun), and Ringo.

One of the humvees outside Firebase Gecko. M2 heavy-barrel
.50-caliber MG and AT4 antitank rockets up top.

Afghan police around Kandahar.

A man they caught with hand grenades and a machine gun in Kandahar. He was released.

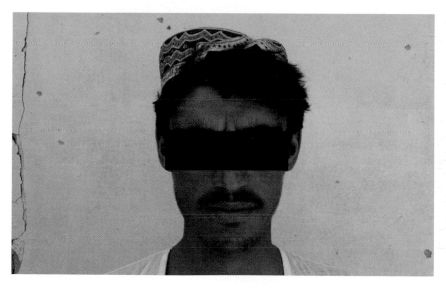

A local who worked for Beast 85 as an interpreter.

A 122mm rocket aimed at downtown Kandahar. The Taliban would aim the rocket, stick a fuse in the back (visible), and then put the fuse in the middle of an insect coil, which takes about two hours to burn down.

This LMTV full of 122mm rockets was captured and is being moved to a location outside of Firebase Gecko to be destroyed.

Here, setting up the same rockets to be destroyed.

Two tons of 122mm rockets explode.

A member of HIG, an outlawed political organization that was
fighting the coalition forces. He joined the Afghan army and then
betrayed them by attacking the U.S. base at Kandahar Airfield. Several
Afghan soldiers were killed while capturing him. He was executed by
the Afghans, and his body was hung up as a warning to others.

Red wears his festive shirt on the occasion of paying the Afghan security forces at Firebase Gecko.

Their "Go-Packs" of ammunition that they could grab and run with. Firebase Gecko.

The captain, Rock, Bubble Boy, and Flipper during mission planning for a raid on a compound in Helmand province.

After being captured, Mullah Osmani is processed for movement to Kandahar Airfield's detention center at Firebase Gecko.

Mullah Osmani in Sangin, Helmand province, on the night of his capture.

Kev flexing outside Kandahar Airfield, June 2002.

May 2002, at Kandahar Airfield.

# *Virginia GuardPost*

### www.virginiaguard.com

| VOLUME XXIV, NO. 6 | SERVING THE ARMY AND AIR GUARD OF VIRGINIA | WINTER 2003 |

# Virginia Special Forces soldiers return from Afghanistan duty

**By Maj. Cotton Puryear**
**Deputy Public Affairs Officer**

Virginia Gov. Mark Warner and Maj. Gen. Claude A. Williams, the adjutant general of Virginia, recently joined family members of soldiers from Company B, 3rd Battalion, 20th Special Forces Group (Airborne) to welcome the soldiers back to Virginia after returning from Afghanistan in early November.

The soldiers had been deployed in support of Operation Enduring Freedom, America's response to the terrorist attacks on September 11, 2001. The soldiers of Company B were mobilized for active federal service in January of 2002.

Company B was initially assigned to the United States Special Forces Command at Fort Bragg, N.C. from January to April 2002. In late April, the unit was attached to 2nd Battalion, 3rd Special Forces Group (Airborne) with the mission of supporting and conducting unconventional warfare operations in Afghanistan and the USCENTCOM area of responsibility.

During five months of continuous

*Photo by Staff Sgt. Mark Turney, VaNG Public Affairs Office*

**Max watches anxiously for his father, Adam, to be released near the end of the ceremonies welcoming home the soldiers of Company B, 3rd Battalion, 20th Special Forces Group.**

unconventional warfare combat and support operations in Afghanistan, Qatar, the Oman and Djibouti, unit leaders said that Company B successfully executed over 100 separate combat missions and numerous staff support activities.

Please see **SF RETURN** on page 3

# New year brings new mobilizations

**By Lt. Col. Chester C. Carter, III**
**Public Affairs Officer**

The new year has brought a wave of new mobilization orders for National Guard units all over the Commonwealth.

Maj. Gen. Claude A. Williams, the adjutant general of Virginia, announced several new mobilization orders during the last weeks of December and first weeks of January. The orders include soldiers of the 189th Engineer Company located in Big Stone Gap, Va. , the 222nd Support Detachment located in Staunton, Va., the 229th Engineer Battalion located in Fredricksburg, Va., the 111th ADA Battalion located in Norfolk, Va.

These mobilizations will be in support of Operation Noble Eagle, the United States' response to the terrorist attacks of September 11, 2001.

Williams said the soldiers from the alerted units would undergo pre-mobilization processing at their home armories and Ft. Pickett prior to deploying to the mobilization stations. After approximately two to three weeks of training at their mobilization stations, the units would deploy to their duty stations.

The soldiers will be ordered to active federal service for a period of one year. The Secretary of the Army may extend this period an additional 12 months based on operation needs or other requirements.

**Please see Page 4 for a complete list of current and completed unit mobilizations from the past year.**

security force of about 30 Hazaras waiting for them, courtesy of the notoriously two-faced Jan Mohammed.

A reinforced rifle platoon from the 82nd Airborne was arriving in a week or two to provide firebase defense and a quick-reaction force, freeing the men up to get out and into the great wide open. It was Beast 85's task to shore up the defenses of the firebase, establish a base security plan, unpack, get local contractors in to start to improve the buildings, set in electric wiring . . . the list went on and on.

Before long, Captain Alan started feeling like shit. He had been feverish and was becoming delirious the night they moved into Deh Rawod. T.T. Boy, who had been driving with the captain, said Red should take a look at him. They got him into his room, put him into bed, and started an IV.

Doc Hoss, the medic, came up and said the captain's fever was 103.5. If it went up another degree, they would have to call in a chopper. Doc Hoss poured both Motrin and Tylenol into the captain. Standing over him in his adobe room, Red felt the heat coming off of his head. He was like a human space heater, sweating like a man in a sauna. The next day, the captain was still fighting a bug, visiting the shitter three times an hour. But thankfully, his fever had broken.

On their second day, the local administrator came to visit them with his entourage of thugs. He worked for Jan Mohammed. If Jan was dirty, this guy was twice as bad. He was Taliban. He could not possibly survive in a town like Deh Rawod if he was on the side of the Americans. He walked into the compound and sat down to drink tea and chat.

Hank, the commander of Beast 63, spoke to the local leader. It sounded like he was in a high-school play, talking in lofty prose about the friendship between the United States and the Afghans, smiling broadly, staring the Taliban thug straight in the eye like he meant it. He came across as a sissy.

Maybe there are times to be soft, but this was not one them. The Deh Rawod locals eat people like Hank for lunch.

Hank should have made the necessary introductions, then gotten down to business with quiet strength and earnestness. He should have grabbed this guy by the balls and laid down the law: if local electricians, plumbers, cooks, and cleaners continued to deny Americans service because of threats, or if they were attacked, it was his neck, and if he didn't start handing over the Taliban, his ass was theirs.

Instead, Hank chose to jerk this guy off—a guy who was making a fortune on their backs on rent and the security force. Red wanted to puke as they left the meeting.

Then came a whole new, cumbersome set of restrictions on operations from the firebase to make matters worse. The rules were laid down by the FOB and the CJSOTF. First, they had to define a 10-kilometer circle around which they had relative free-dom of movement. For all operations within the 10 kilometers they would have to submit a 5-W form (who, what, when, where, and why). It would first have to go through the B-team, then the FOB. The catch was that a 5-W could only be approved if it was considered "routine." Missions beyond the 10-kilometer circle, or any that involved combat operations, required approval from the B-team, FOB, and CJSOTF, and then the Combined Task Force. Approval for a 5-W could take 6 hours, a CONOP as long as 48.

To Red and the others, the whole process was a waste of valuable time, and wasting time is not what special forces was designed for. Red was growing sick and tired of all this, so he started cheating. He plotted a 15- to 20-kilometer circle around the firebase and submitted the points as the 10-kilometer limits of the 5-Ws. Then he did something even more clever. He plotted most of the major road intersections around the firebase as reference points and waypoints for vehicle travel. By giving the FOB the coordinates for reference, they could put together the required paperwork for the Battalion S3 to approve more quickly.

Most of the time 5-Ws or CONOPs were denied for trivial reasons. It could be obvious as hell what the team in the field was requesting, but the CONOP or the 5-W would get hung up on a minor point of format. This self-imposed insanity encouraged people to hide in their firebases and avoid missions altogether.

The new rules would soon be tested. As dusk fell on that second day, a truck carrying a group of men armed to the teeth stopped in the open desert outside their gate about a kilometer from the firebase. A member of the local militia standing near Red pointed and said "al Qaeda." He had a serious look on his face.

That was enough for Captain Alan, who ordered Stitch and Ringo to kit up and take a couple vehicles up to the front gate. They were going to stop the truck and see what those guys wanted. As they pulled up behind the gate, Hank walked over and asked them what they were doing. Red told him while passing.

He said, "Now, not so fast." (*Goddammit*, Red thought, *did that sound familiar*.) He wanted to know if they had sent up a CONOP or a 5-W to the FOB for approval!

If that's how it had to be, then fine, but there was no time to waste. They requested permission in a text message sent by radio to the AOB commander. They asked nicely if it would be possible to leave the front gate of the firebase and proceed 1 kilometer due south, within plain view of the compound to investigate a suspicious truck filled with armed men casing the firebase. Then they waited . . . and waited . . . and waited, for minutes on end.

Fucking madness.

By the time it was approved an hour later, the al Qaeda truck had moved on.

The team sergeant from Beast 63 walked over to Red and said, "Hey, this was not what we are here for, not right now." He'd been deployed for about eight months. Red got the distinct impression that he was happy just biding time before rotating back to the States.

If they were not here to give chase to al Qaeda right now, why *were* they here?

Four days later, the 82nd Airborne platoon landed outside the compound with the rifle platoon they had been promised. They landed four CH-47s, with two Apache attack helicopters circling overhead. As soon as the Chinooks landed, the 82nd Airborne guys came running out of the backs of the birds and lay down in a circle. They were in full battle rattle, and they were hot. The men moved themselves and their supplies into the left compound of the firebase, same as Beast 85's.

With the security platoon in place, they could now start operating outside the firebase. The first thing on Red and the other men of Beast 85's minds was to drive to the location of their objectives for the Full Throttle mission. They drove to the river and crossed at a major ford site to the north of the objective. They followed the road along the western side of the river and south toward the objectives. About 5 kilometers from the village, the road ended, so they drove around the Sart'oghay Mountains and took a valley west of the Helmand to the south of the objective. Then they jumped on a road there and headed north.

Then that road ended. Through an interpreter, a local kid told them that there was no road to the village of Sart'oghay. The 3rd Group team had told them that they had driven the road past the objective. Red looked down as the road narrowed to a donkey trail that a guy on a dirt bike could drive on. A truck could have never driven any farther north on that road. The 3rd Group teams had never driven past the objective. It was another fucking dangerous lie.

Had they even been able to ford the river the night of Full Throttle—the bullshit location they'd been given of the ford site—they would have stalled about 5 kilometers south of the objective. The helicopters that were going to bring the 19th Group guys in might have committed to landing with the false assurance that they were going to be close behind. It also turned out that they would have faced antiaircraft artillery in the area of the objective.

A week into Beast 85's stay at the firebase, the company commander and the company operations sergeant, Al, moved from Tarin Kowt into the compound. The C Company commander and Al got along with the men well. They shared evening meals and enjoyed discussing the ways of the National Guard and what they did in the outside world.

Two weeks in, the FOB dropped a "bomb" on the men. C Company had teams on the Pakistani border. They were doing nothing except sending 5-Ws and CONOPs, which were systematically delayed or rejected. An idea to move Charlie Company off to another area had been scrapped. Instead, the entire company would move to the Helmand area. Charlie Company, a 3rd Group company, was moving in, while Bravo Company, with Beast 85 (along with Beast 83 in Tarin Kowt) was moving out. Beast 65 was going to replace Beast 85, who was subsequently going to head back to Kandahar Airfield, sit in the dust, and do nothing.

The "summer help" had already taken care of the manual labor. Red, the captain, and the others had done all the hard work on the base improvements, set up the firebase with a security platoon, worked out a resupply plan, established a firebase defense plan, and worked out all the required administrative details to conduct offensive operations. The table was set, and a 3rd Group team was going to come on in and take their place. Some fucking gratitude.

Red pondered the process that led to the decision to move Beast 85. The FOB commander was in charge of the southern half of the country and had three special forces line companies to utilize. There were some obvious holes in 3rd SFGA's coverage of the border, some deliberate, others not. The main road from Kandahar to Pakistan was through Spin Buldak, which had no team. This was al Qaeda's highway and there was no U.S. check post.

There were other examples. Senior al Qaeda and Taliban leaders were known to be hiding in places like Deh Rawod and the central-northern highlands. In the Deh Rawod area alone, three high-value targets were suspected to be lurking around. They had a fair amount of intelligence about their location, but they were not allowed to go after them. Nothing made sense. He felt sick, disoriented, and exhausted. One more week here and then back to Kandahar, where they'd only be fighting each other out of frustration and boredom.

Red went to Charlie Company's commander and asked him what was going on. He flatly told him the decision had been made at the FOB and approved by the CJSOTF to move Charlie Company into the Helmand area. He said he had not asked for the move and agreed that it would mean a loss in momentum in any offensive operations. It would take weeks before the new teams would be ready to begin meaningful operations.

Red returned from recon one day to find that the rest of B-team had moved from Tarin Kowt and was now on their side of the compound. Sergeant Major Trails, who had also moved from Tarin Kowt to Deh Rawod, wanted to push Red out so two specialist mechanics could move into his tiny room. In the meantime, he wanted Red to double up with them until the move was complete. There was no way two people could sleep in that little mudroom.

This time, Red snapped. He tracked down Trails again and told him his leadership was insane. Why were they even bothering to fight? Why were they wasting all this energy on administrative burdens if hunting al Qaeda and the Taliban was really their priority? And if they were being booted out of Deh Rawod, then Red would have no choice but to fly back to Kandahar tomorrow on the resupply helicopter and find a new home for his team. Then he stormed off to bed, leaving Trails speechless.

Red kept his word, and the next morning rode a CH-47 back to Kandahar Airfield. A 19-hour trip by vehicle took only 90 minutes by helicopter. The air was cool, and the view was brilliant. The Valley of the Children was an astonishing sight to behold from above. The CH-47 landed on the runway at Kandahar. Red immediately headed to the FOB to find someone else to yell at.

He found their company commander, who was not sympathetic to his complaints. Quite the contrary. As far as he was concerned, Beast 83 and 85 had been stolen from him, and now he was happy to have them back. He had been selling the FOB on the idea of a mobile AOB for special forces company staff. The mobile base would head out into the wild blue yonder with the A- and B-teams. The B-team would set up a mission-support site in the desert and push teams out on long-duration patrols along the southern border.

In other words, Bravo Company would load up and run around the desert for three months. Moreover, since there would be no aircraft or aerial resupply, the men would have to return to the base if supplies or fuel ran out.

Red was pissed, and it showed.

But something was about to happen that would change the rest of the deployment for Beast 85. Firebase Gecko, just north of Kandahar, in Mullah Omar's old compound, was freeing up. Nineteenth SFGA was there with an AOB in Kandahar City, but they were moving back to their FOB in preparation to redeploy back to the States. FOB 32 was given the firebase and tasked Beast 85's company commander to pick a team to move to Gecko.

Upon hearing this, Red was determined to get Beast 85 out to Gecko. Then he got sick.

It started on the trip to Kandahar. Two days later, he was unable to get out of bed. He felt as if his body had been sucked under a steamroller and crushed into small sharp pieces. He was unable to eat, unable to get out of his cot. He had put his gear in the far corner of an empty tent and was in a sleeping bag shivering and sweating. "Roger," another guy from their company who had just shown up from the States, peeked in and asked how he was doing. Red croaked to him in a strained voice that he needed a medic.

Thirty minutes later, Red was lying in the hospital at the main terminal by the airfield. Two IVs with antibiotics were running, while at the same time they were sucking out his blood. He was told to stay in the hospital until the doctors could figure out what was going on with him, but the hospital was hot, the cots were uncomfortable, and they were building something just behind the ward. All he could hear was the constant bang, bang, banging of hammers.

Red spent a day suffering in the hospital, and then, determined to get his team to Firebase Gecko, he simply got up, walked out, and went back to his dark, cool tent to sleep for two full days. He lost about 10 pounds that week. The antibiotics began to work, and he felt well enough to get up and get to work.

Gecko was located to the north of Kandahar, about a 45-minute drive from the front gate of Kandahar Airfield. Nineteenth SFGA had an advanced operations base in Kandahar City proper. They had a B-team and three A-teams in and around the Kandahar area. One was at Gecko.

The firebase occupied the northern tip of Mullah Omar's compound just north of Kandahar proper. Early in the war, when DELTA Force had raided the compound, AC-130s destroyed every building but Mullah Omar's residence. They raided the compound in an impressive air assault, but missed Omar, who had headed to the hills. Gecko had a range that special operations teams used. The team lived in buildings that had plumbing and utility power from Kandahar. The rest of the 19th Group guys lived in the governor's compound in the center of the city. It was a nice, comfortable place by Afghan standards, with a green garden and lots of room.

Unlike 3rd SFGA, which concentrated their teams along the Pakistani border, 19th Group stuck to the population centers, which is where most intelligence originated. They had teams in Mazar-i-Sharif, Jalalabad, Herat, and Kandahar. They worked directly with the Afghans and were a lot more successful in their efforts.

Nineteenth Group was pulling out of Kandahar to position the advanced operations base in Uzbekistan for redeployment back to the United States. They had no plans to replace the team with another. They gave the area to 3rd SFGA, and 3rd SFGA was going to give it to Bravo Company. All of Bravo Company's teams, except Beast 83 and 85, were still being used in staff positions. It looked like they were going to land in Gecko, take over from the 19th Group guys, and start doing some meaningful work.

Flipper and Red drove out to the 19th Group advanced operations base in the governor's palace in downtown Kandahar, hoping that 19th Group would let them take over. But before that could happen, he witnessed an incredible exercise in political maneuvering—U.S. Army style.

Nineteenth Group was hoping that 3rd Group would replace the AOB with their B-team and four A-teams and continue what the 19th Group had done. But the 3rd Group commander said, "No way!" He wasn't going to give up the 24 ASTs languishing in the FOB headquarters and let them go out and fight the enemy. He wanted them at headquarters, not in the field. Only one team would go to Gecko—end of story. The rest of the company would work out of Kandahar.

The governor of Kandahar province was pissed. As one of the most powerful governors in the country, Shirzai knew a lot about what was going on in the southern half of Afghanistan. He was a source of a lot of intelligence. Plus, with several generals and chiefs of intelligence, the police, and several thousand Afghan soldiers all in the greater Kandahar region, a lot of intel was floating around. Nineteenth Group had used its contacts well to gather intelligence about the enemy and had conducted several high-profile military operations with the Afghans that netted thousands of pounds of explosives and weapons. Kandahar was a treasure trove of intelligence as well as a strategic center in southern Afghanistan. The governor wanted a company of special forces in the town, not a single team. It gave him prestige in the eyes of his friends and enemies, and provided a degree of security for him.

Third Group told him sorry, they were going to have only one team out at Gecko, and that was that. Red started to fear that they would send some other team, but Flipper, who loved Beast 85, proposed his favorite team for the Gecko mission. And Major S., who also liked them, thought it might be good to get Beast 85 back on its feet. It was down to two options, Beast 83 and Beast 85, for the mission. The battalion commander recommended Beast 85.

Deh Rawod was the best game in Afghanistan and a huge boost to their morale. Now they were going to move out to Gecko the second week of August and start conducting real missions. They were on a roll.

Beast 85 set up a temporary space in the forward-base tent city and started the transition with 19th Group AOB. The next two weeks involved working with their teams to understand the complexities of the politico-military environment in and around Kandahar City. The meetings were highly informative.

Although Kandahar Airfield had the second-largest concentration of U.S. forces in the country, few people ever left the base during their entire six-month rotation. Kandahar Airfield was an island. The city of Kandahar was about 15 kilometers away, but it may as well have been 1,000 kilometers. The men had to understand the workings and personalities of the people in town to be successful, and no one in 3rd SFGA or 20th SFGA knew anything about Kandahar.

Beast 85 mapped out flow charts of Afghan leadership in Kandahar, Helmand, and Zabul provinces with 19th Group's area operations base commander and his operations guys. These guys knew their subject well, and Beast 85 was going to be the only A-team working the entire southern part of the country. The other three teams would keep making photocopies at FOB 32. It turned out that Helmand and Zabul provinces were being run by Pashtuns who were playing both sides of the fence. The two provinces were a treasure trove of Taliban weapons and munitions, and soon Beast 85 would have them at their disposal.

CHAPTER **12**

# FIREBASE GECKO

Beast 85's spirits were reasonably high when they moved into Gecko on 14 August 2002. The firebase occupied the northern tip of Mullah Omar's compound. The compound was roomy and was shaped like a huge diamond pointing north and south. There were about 20 structures in the place, most of them flattened by the heavy fighting a few months earlier. Along the northern tip of the compound was a series of single-story structures, built of brick, not adobe, into the eastern wall. Right at the tip was a rook-like circular building that was an obvious guard tower. Just to the left of the rook and still along the wall was another building.

There was room for the guys to live comfortably, to set up an operations center, provide a room for the interpreters, and store all their ammo. The 19th Group guys had built an ammunition supply point, a mortar pit, a bunker to run to if they were shelled, and a guard tower. The place only needed a well so the men wouldn't have to rely on the Afghan army to truck in water, and they were going to make that their priority base-improvement project.

The camp came with a full Afghan staff. They had four interpreters, one engineer, one cook, one cleaning boy, and 12 security guards on the payroll, but who were on loan from the Afghan 2nd

Corps, and a 2nd Corps Liaison, who spied on the camp for his corps commander. Otherwise, they were fairly reliable.

The locals that worked for them were generally young men who all spoke English—except for the security force. They were all students, at what might be considered high-school level. They came from middle-class families. The youngest interpreter was 17, and the oldest was 25. They loved all things American: M&Ms, Eminem, Beyonce, Oreo cookies, everything.

Beast 85 treated them well, gave them their own room in the compound, a DVD player and television set, and a working air conditioner. They asked three of them to be at work during the day and at least one at night. When they accompanied the men on missions, they wore body armor and Kevlar helmets, but could not have a weapon.

Red and the others suspected they were reporting back to someone, but not the Taliban. The men were pretty relaxed around them, but were sure not to give them any operational details.

Gecko had one room that was totally off limits to all non-team personnel, Afghan or otherwise—the operational center. If they caught an Afghan trying to go in the OPCEN, or even show-ing curiosity about what was going on inside, they would fire him. The rules were clearly laid down, and the Afghan staff followed them.

The engineer was responsible for the plumbing and electri-cal plant at the firebase. He was a tall, strange guy who would boss the other Afghans around. The Afghan cook was from New York City. He had stepped on a Russian mine as a kid and had a huge scar on his left ankle. He had moved to New York, but years later he had come home to Kandahar for a visit and got swept up in the Taliban occupation. He spoke English with a strong New

York accent. He loved New York City and was saving every penny to return there. The cleaning boy was a tall, lanky guy who swept the patios, cleaned the bathrooms, and burned the trash. It was a good crew of guys. The men enjoyed great rapport with them, and they even helped morale.

On the second night at Gecko, after watching a DVD, Red got up to take a piss. His urine was bright red. The blood in his urine couldn't possibly have been from his earlier bout with typhoid. He showed the medic his urine sample, who took him to see the doctors at Kandahar Airfield 45 minutes away. They reviewed his history, including all the antibiotics he had been given. There was a possibility that the cause was a rare but serious side effect of the high dose of antibiotics doctors had previously given him.

They had him medevac'd to Germany for a closer look.

Germany was green, cool, and had no dust. The hospital staff set Red up in a nice room in the base hotel. He got a pass for food at the chow hall. They brought him civilian clothes to wear. He was dirty, and he had not shaved or cut his hair in four months. Red had left Afghanistan dirty and with only the clothes on his back. In no time, his hair was combed, his beard washed and neatened, and his tattered uniform exchanged for shiny new duds.

Red got the full workup: MRI, CAT scan, blood work, consultation with a urologist, and medication. All his appointments were in the morning, and they were finished by 1000 hours, so he had almost the entire day off. The coordinator said he would stay there at least 10 days before he could return to duty—or even home to the States.

So Red got on the phone, called his wife Lorie, and had her book the next flight to Germany. She left their kids with her sister and jumped on a plane to Frankfurt. The two of them met at the international arrivals section. She looked at Red, then past him, then around him. It was clear she didn't recognize her husband. After all, he was a good 30 pounds slimmer than when she last saw him, and had a beard.

Lorie hated the beard.

The two of them checked into a local hotel to spend the next four days relaxing, eating, and seeing the sights. They discussed the possibility of Red being cleared to return to the United States. He told Lorie he was going to return to the team regardless of what the doctors told him. He had to see this thing through, and anyway, if he returned to the States he would have to spend three months on staff duty at Fort Bragg.

The tests were completed, and the diagnosis was kidney stones and typhoid fever. The air force doctor in charge told him that he was going to indeed recommend his return to the States, insisting that there was no way Red should be allowed back in Afghanistan. Red's body was seriously worn down, and a firebase in the middle of some wasteland was definitely not the place to cure kidney stones or typhoid.

Sit out the war with his team still in country? The hell with that!

So Red hitched a ride to Rhein-Main Air Base, filled a duffel bag with as much hard liquor as he could carry, and hopped the next C-17 back to Kandahar.

He called the team on his way and arranged for them to pick him up when he landed. When he did, they feted him like a rock star.

There wasn't much time to party, though. The team was to go out on a mission that same night.

They were going to be in search of an HIG (an outlaw terrorist group aligned with the Taliban) meeting on the outskirts of Kandahar. They had received the mission from their friends at the CIA, who had followed them to Gecko. One of their informants had told them about the meeting and was given a GPR. He was told to go to the compound where the meeting was being held and push the waypoint button on the GPR, then bring the GPR back to them. The idea was to get a set of coordinates for the target compound. They were to drive to find the target, kick in the door, and bag the bad guys.

The Afghan 3rd Commando, a group of about a hundred Afghans funded, armed, and fed by the United States, rarely did anything without Beast 85. Rock, a SWAT cop from New Jersey, worked with them three days a week and even started to think of them as his children. The 3rd Commando guys loved Rock. He called them "strikers." All Rock had to say was "strikers," and the Afghans would jump up and down. He was their Colonel Kurtz from *Apocalypse Now*, an almost cultlike father figure to them.

Operations used to have to be approved by the forward base and the special ops task force clowns in Bagram, but now things had changed. Until recently, whenever they wanted to drive to Kandahar to pick up mail, it was a CONOP. If they wanted to meet the governor—which they needed to do every day—it was a CONOP. If they did anything, it was a CONOP. Captain Alan had fought over this with FOB 32 while Red was in Germany. He'd asked that greater Kandahar be designated a 5-W area, and requested that they only be required to submit a CONOP when they were going on a mission.

A majority of the day-to-day travel they did around Kandahar was meeting with the local political and military leadership. Groups were constantly going out of the firebase to the same routine meetings, every stinking day.

Captain Alan managed to get around this madness. At first, the FOB always insisted that it wanted CONOPs for each of the meetings. The captain said if they wanted CONOPs then they would get CONOPs. The FOB started getting 10 CONOPs a day requesting permission to do routine things. The captain was following their rules, and the FOB was starting to choke on the tidal wave of CONOPs he sent them. The FOB in turn sent their requests to the CJSOTF in Bagram, and Bagram started wondering what the hell was happening down south. It was the only way to make them change their mind.

The FOB waved the white flag. The men could operate with only a 5-W within a 20-mile radius. Trips to Kandahar were included. The problem was that Red could never get them to call it official policy. FOB wanted the CONOPs in their back pocket as a weapon against too much efficiency on their part. They could always ask, "Did you submit your CONOP?"

As Red typed up his CONOP, or 5-W, for the FOB over the tactical satellite channel, the team started its internal mission planning. They relied on SOPs more than anything else. They couldn't depend on the on-the-ground descriptions of the targets because they always changed. They war-gamed the plan and made a terrain model. Once they went into the target it would be all SOP. The 3rd Commando's participation was relative to the size of the target. They were on the initial breach team and would be some of the first into the target.

Having sent the CONOP, the men loaded their gear onto the vehicles, checked the radios, briefed the mission, and rolled out the gates. They had the coordinates of the HIG compound, which was described as an inn of some type.

The HIG was going to be having a big regional meeting. The men had plotted the coordinates on a map of the Kandahar area, and the location appeared to be slightly out of town. They drove through Kandahar heading south, picking their way along the narrow streets, always trying to point themselves toward the target coordinates. They drove for a few hours until they had made their way to the outskirts of the city, and they found themselves in an open field. There was a compound, but it was small, with no vehicles outside, and no meeting taking place inside. If there had been, they would have seen their guards and vehicles.

The men dismounted and walked toward the purported exact location of the inn—and found only an empty farm field with an irrigation ditch near the coordinates. Their CIA friends had received flawed intelligence. Red wondered if they had paid the snitch enough.

He and the others returned to Gecko. The next day, he drove an ATV to the larger compound where the CIA team was located to introduce himself and make fun of them. The leader of the group, nicknamed "Agent Smith," turned out to be a really nice, clever guy who was fully capable and aware of the realities they worked with. Beast 85 quickly established a good working relationship with Agent Smith and the other operatives. Best of all, they had beer.

Beast 85 provided security for them, and in return, they shared some intelligence with them. If they had something in the Kandahar area they wanted exploited, Beast 85 was usually given the right of first refusal to knock it down. This was a case of perfect strategic fit.

# CHAPTER 13

# THE CAPTURE OF OSMANI

*The following is an account of the operation to capture Mullah Akhtar Mohammed Osmani, during which time Red remained back at Gecko.*

From mid-August to mid-October, Beast 85 finally found its place in Afghanistan and started to go after the enemy. They built on the foundations 19th Group had started and quickly set a routine of going out and meeting the political and military leaders, gathering intelligence, and then going out on combat missions to exploit the intelligence. Because of their physical proximity with the CIA agents and because of the great rapport they enjoyed with them, Beast 85 was starting to get some really solid, actionable intelligence.

The captain's only fear was that, after having wasted more than three months of their time, the Bagram fools would send them back to the States without allowing them to bag anything or anyone. Beast 85 was determined not to allow that to happen. If that meant breaking some rules, then they would break them.

Within the greater Kandahar region they worked with the following men:

**Gul Agha Shirzai**, the governor of Kandahar province and the military commander for the southern military district of Afghanistan. He was one of the two or three most powerful men in the Afghan political game.

**Khalid Pashtun**, political adviser to the governor. He was an American citizen who used to sell cars in New Mexico. He was an opportunist who worked both sides of the game for personal power and wealth.

**Khan Mohammed**, the 2nd Corps commander of the Afghan Military Force. He reported to Shirzai, but was appointed to President Karzai.

**Red Gulalai (a.k.a. "General Slappy")**, 540th Brigade commander under Khan Mohammed. He was hard to read.

**General Gulalai**, chief of the Office of Civil Intelligence (OCI) in the southern military district. He was a tough, mean, hard man who seemed to have been fighting someone his entire adult life. Beast 85 worked with him more than anyone else. He was the source of a lot of solid, actionable intelligence he'd earned the hard way—although he was later fired over human rights abuses.

**Haji Abdullah Khan**, an influential political figure and a potential future candidate for the presidency.

**General Akram**, chief of police for Kandahar. Akram was the fattest Afghan the captain had met. He didn't get along with General Gulalai or any of the Civil Intelligence people. Beast 85 had trouble managing this conflict. Because he knew they were friends with General Gulalai, they didn't work together as much as they should have.

**Pacha Shirzai**, cousin of the governor and head of security for Kandahar Airfield. Since Beast 85 got along well with Agha Shirzai, they were friends with Pacha, too.

**Colonel Engineer**, OCI intelligence officer. A good guy and a great source of intelligence, iron hand in a velvet glove.

**Jan Mohammed**, the governor of Uruzgan province. He was crooked.

**Shir Mohammed**, the governor of Helmand province. He despised Americans and vouched for the Taliban. He was appointed by President Karzai, but hated by all in the province who were not drug smugglers or Taliban supporters.

Each member of Beast 85 was assigned a man from the list to meet with about events in the country and the region several times each week. The meetings were formal at first, but since they met week after week, they become more relaxed, and the Afghans would bring back juicy gossip and intelligence on the southern region.

A lot of the intel dealt with the internal politics that permeated Afghan culture. They are terribly loyal to their ethnic group, clan, and subclan. It was like the Hatfields and McCoys times a thousand. The men were told on more than one occasion to be careful not to pit one clan against another under the guise of going after the Taliban. Special forces teams had been fooled into helping clans settle old scores early on in the war with close air support.

The OCI turned into the greatest single source of intelligence for the detachment during its stay at Gecko. General Gulalai wanted to work with them to catch the Taliban, so he made an effort to use his agents to gather information that they would like. He had a personal agenda, unmistakably. Gulalai could gain access to areas in southern Afghanistan he could never hope to get into without Beast 85's presence there.

Once he moved past Kandahar province, his men would be shot at by the military of the surrounding provinces. If they were with the detachment, they could get into places to extract payback for something that had nothing to do with their mission. It happened a few times. The detachment had a deal with him.

Captain Alan had Stitch and Spidey, his two trained intelligence guys, go out to the OCI with a chief warrant officer in military intelligence every day. They would return, and the group would pore over the intelligence. The chief, Jake, was reporting to the 82nd Airborne and the combined joint task force (CJTF) in Bagram. Jake was a great person to work with. They avoided any turf wars by combining resources and recognizing that they were all on the same side. Jake had five guys in his compound, and Beast 85 went on missions with them all the time.

The detachment allowed Jake to do the interrogations of anyone they nabbed. Of course, if they brought every guy they grabbed to the detention center at Kandahar Airfield, it would have become unmanageable. Instead, they would round up the Taliban and al Qaeda on an objective, and if Jake were there he would have a little talk with them to decide who got to be a "guest of the United States" at Guantanamo.

The benefit of working with the local population and leadership is that information comes to you as it might in any other hometown gossip session. As the people that Beast 85 worked with became more comfortable with them, so increased their desire to be part of their successes as Americans and soldiers.

They knew that special forces men were different from the average soldiers that moved together in herds, passing briefly through their villages and cities on their way to somewhere else but ultimately destined to load up on the big silver freedom bird and leave Afghanistan behind without a further thought. Special forces uses the word *rapport*, but that doesn't begin to describe the unique connection that they feel with the indigenous forces they recruit, train, and fight alongside.

Captain Alan's 18F, Stitch, was his point man with the OCI and its controversial leader General Haji Gulalai. While General Gulalai was appointed by President Karzai to be the intelligence chief of Kandahar City, he turned stepping on the toes of everyone, all the way up to Karzai himself, into an art form. Every day, Stitch would go down to OCI and sit for hours as Gulalai went through pages and pages of intelligence reports.

In the captain's meetings with other members of the government, it was apparent that the fact that they were paying Gulalai so much attention really made them nervous. In particular, Governor Gul Agha Shirzai and his right-hand man, Khalid Pashtun, spent a lot of time trying to discourage them from acting on OCI intelligence without first consulting them. In fact, the sheer volume of information that came out of Gulalai's office meant that they could not possibly go chasing around the countryside after every tip and tidbit of his information. Sorting through the garbage and extrapolating something that resembled an enemy situation template required Jake's added expertise.

The team leader of the military intelligence/counterintelligence detachment located at Beast 85's firebase, Jake was as indispensable as any member of the Gecko team. Every day, first thing in the morning, Ringo, Stitch, and Jake would load up the SUV nicknamed "Turtle" because of its mushy diesel engine and head down to OCI for a three-to-four-hour download with Gulalai and his lieutenant, Colonel Engineer. Hours of drinking caffeine-laced chai tea and Pakistani sugar candies was like throwing gasoline on the fire of Stitch's already manic personality.

By the time Stitch returned to the firebase, he would be so hopped-up on sugar and caffeine that he would rip through a stream-of-consciousness debrief of what he had covered with the general over the previous four hours, blast the captain with raw data, making him feel like he was drinking from a fire hose, and then disappear into his room. Once inside, his body would shut down and he would crash for several hours until he awoke in the afternoon for mission prep and operations. In the meantime, a tag team of Chief and Ringo would decipher and extrapolate the information that Stitch had gathered.

While it sounds convoluted, it worked. Each had his role in the three-man tag team of OCI. For all his bizarre hyperactivity and absolute refusal to provide the captain with a finished intelligence product, Stitch had incredible rapport with the OCI crew. As the detachment's role in the war became more and more reliant upon intelligence gathered at their level, Stitch would delve into the depths of maintaining rapport with General Gulalai and his soldiers, almost to the point of going native on the captain.

Beast 85 began to compile information on the location of one of the most-wanted members of the Taliban regime. Mullah Akhtar Mohammed Osmani was 2nd Corps commander under the Taliban, and acting military chief since November 2001. From the Musa Quelah district of the Kandahar province, he had fallen off the intelligence radar. But there was now credible information and an agent willing to take Beast 85 to Osmani. Though the captain was dubious at first, he began planning.

Information had a top-down flow at the battalion level. The "big brains" on the staff planned future operations to dovetail into current operations as much as possible to achieve a coherent campaign strategy. The battalion commander (BC) would be advised by his staff on the current situation, proposed operations, and targets. Once approved by the BC, the operations order would go to the respective detachments. Those teams would then plan their part in the operation.

In planning the operation to track down Osmani, they came to Beast 85 for answers. They would develop the plan, ferret out the information, judge its validity, and check the reliability of its source. To a large extent, they were flying solo.

After experiencing what came to be known as the "limp-dick memo," Beast 85 was careful about the information they passed up through the chain of command. The memo had come down through the forward operations base from the CJSOTF in Bagram. It spelled out the intent of the CJSOTF commander and his staff:

> *No direct action operations.*
> *No death and/or destruction.*
> *Stay in the firebases unless there is clearly no*
> *danger of getting into a shooting match.*
> *Keep your heads down, and*
> *For God's sake, don't take any risks.*

The effect of such a wimpy order only provoked the men to seek even more high adventure.

Beast 85 conducted operations under the label of "route reconnaissance" and "area assessment" for about a month and a half, and they became quite successful, both at catching the Taliban and al Qaeda operatives and their equipment, and at flying below the CJSOTF radar screen. By fudging the aggressive and overly restrictive guidelines set up by the clowns at Bagram, which would otherwise have delayed their missions, they managed to go out on 45 missions, capture three high-value targets, and destroy tens of thousands of pounds of ammunition.

This included catching the Taliban minister of passports (the third-ranking high-value target), and Mullah Rafiq, a key Taliban commander. During their stay in Afghanistan, no one else caught a single high-value target. This wasn't because special forces didn't want to fight, but because their missions were systematically delayed or cancelled by Bagram.

Late one evening, Stitch came to Captain Alan with some very hot intelligence regarding Osmani. Stitch was looking tense, and very excited. Targets like these were prizes for the "special" special forces units, which were groomed to conduct snatch operations and had been spoon-fed planning information. The problem was that they were so groomed and controlled that it was an impossible task for them to seize the initiative from an enemy that was familiar with their tactics. Well versed in their rules of engagement, and adept at melting into the surrounding population at the sound of orbiting AC-130s, low-flying Predator UAVs, and blacked-out spec ops helicopters whop-whopping overhead, the enemy was just not cooperating.

Weeks-long planning cycles, echelons-above-God staff briefings, and the pursuit of the 100 percent solution meant that these units found themselves fast-roping more often than not into abandoned compounds.

If Captain Alan sent up a CONOP with Mullah Osmani's name on it, Beast 85 would be done. The best-case scenario was for him to submit a CONOP, per the CJSOTF SOP, no less than 54 hours prior to the planned conduct of the operation. It would need to include plans for Predator, Spectres, B-52s, fast-movers, up-armored humvees, infantry brigade in blocking positions, and no less than a company on a short string to respond to contact as a quick-reaction force. It would be a typical JTF-180 large-footprint Hollywood-style extravaganza that would guarantee they would find nothing.

Or even more likely, Beast 85 would be told to stand down, and the CJSOTF pukes would use signal intelligence, imagery intelligence, and military intelligence voodoo to confirm and reconfirm before committing their pet unit to a target that days before had become nonexistent. The captain decided Beast 85 would conduct the operation, and Beast 85 would conduct it so that the Taliban and the joint task force would learn of it at about the same time. It was the only way.

Now, the intelligence asset was telling Stitch that Osmani was only days from fleeing to Pakistan to meet up with his Taliban cronies, who were busy trying to choose a new leader to replace Mullah Omar. Word on the street was that the power players had decided that the Taliban needed a new charismatic leader to rally people around their cause in Afghanistan, and Mullah Osmani was on the short list.

Captain Alan and his men were under the gun to get this thing done. He wanted to launch this within 12 hours. Their experience had shown them that they could move on an objective just prior to the first call to prayer at 0430 hours and roll up in their Toyota pickups and traditional Afghan garb without raising much attention. This was critical to keeping the Taliban's early warning system of local shopkeepers, policemen, and government-approved checkpoints from alerting the target to the team's approach.

The objective area was about four hours away. Add an hour to pinpoint the objective and get into position and an hour as a buffer. That meant that Beast 85 had to roll out of the firebase no later than 2300 hours. There would still be a lot of locals out and about, but the sight of Beast 85's pickups departing the firebase accompanied by 3rd Commando pickups was nothing new. They conducted two to three operations each week. There would be no way of telling where they were going at that point. The captain's concern was that the long drive would take them through many checkpoints.

As they got closer to the objective, it would become easier to determine their general objective area. They had to come up with a plan to take the early warning system of checkpoints, police officers, street peddlers, and young men in need of a little financial augmentation from local officials that got paid to protect their tribal brethren who were former Taliban.

Hours of brain-racking and war-gaming went into the plan. They needed to get into the target, and they needed to do it without tipping off the bad guys. Finally they had the idea. They would get a lead element in. They could tell them where the checkpoints were and get onto the target to set in a cordon as they rolled into town. The problem was that by the very nature of the element, it would be very light and very exposed. It would have to hide in plain sight, and walk among the bad guys like nothing was out of the ordinary.

The men would infiltrate a split team . . . no, two guys . . . nah, better have at least four guys. They would infiltrate four guys in the back of a pickup . . . no, in a taxicab . . . yeah, four guys in a taxicab, in jundi-wear and skullcaps (with desert-camouflage uniform bottoms, in accordance with judge advocate general and the rules of engagement, of course) and OCI drivers and passengers mixed in to handle any small talk at check points . . . They could get them into the target, they could use a GPR to give them the location and number of checkpoints, and then set in an undetected cordon a silent stealthy net, around the objective just in case the main body was compromised on infil and the Mullah tried to melt away. If he tried to squirt, the cordon team would roll him up and wait for the cavalry to arrive. It was perfect, it was unapproved, and it was all Beast 85's.

Operation Avril—named after Canadian pop singer Avril Lavigne, who was hot with skateboard punks at the time—was on a roll.

But the men needed the main body to be closer, just in case something went wrong. That way, a quick reaction force could get them out.

So they modified the plan. The lead element would go on as planned, but they would be no farther ahead than 45 to 50 minutes—a long time if you are in the shit, but not as bad as four hours. And they could close the gap if things even started to get squirrelly.

Captain Alan and his men lined up the vehicles in march order inside the compound, and he slipped a CD into the stereo of his converted civilian vehicle. As Eminem rapped, "This looks like a job for me, so ev'rybody just follow me, cause we need a little controversy . . . ," jundis stared awestruck at the wailing truck, and team guys bobbed their heads and rapped along as they conducted their final precombat equipment and mental checks.

The captain surveyed the line to make sure everyone was up. It was surreal, rolling out on a combat operation with their own private army and their own hardcore rap soundtrack. There were no armored humvees with .50-caliber M2 machine guns or MK19 grenade launchers for them to play with. They had long since broken down or been cast aside for the low-signature soft-sided vehicles in their convoy.

• • •

First in order of march was Captain Alan's vehicle, a four-door Toyota Tacoma pickup, call-sign "Shark." Ringo was driving, the captain was riding shotgun, their interpreters "Skippy" and "Li'l Kid" were folded into the back seat, and Rock was flying the rollbar-mounted 240B 7.62mm machine gun while ringed by as many of his strikers from 3rd Commando as they could pack in.

Next came the rented Toyota SUV, call-signed "Turtle" because of its miserably sluggish diesel engine, with Stitch, their intelligence asset, and a man from the military intelligence detachment. Intermingled with team vehicles were the three four-door Toyota Hilux pickups driven and loaded down with jundis from 3rd Commando.

And last, their second Toyota Tacoma Hammer, with Doc riding shotgun. Joe, who they called "Flipper," piloted the machine gun, and a guy from the military intelligence detachment was at the helm. Normally, Flipper would be in one of the Hiluxes to maintain positive control of 3rd Commando, but with the operation calling for a split infiltration, they were running out of special forces guys.

At 1730, several hours after dark, the assault element rolled out of the firebase and down the road to and through Kandahar. Although they were a good-size convoy, only a few people would be on the streets, and suspicions would not be raised.

The cordon element was going through its own trials and tribulations. The plan had called for them to link up with the jundis from the OCI and depart NLT at 1630. That would put them on the road about an hour ahead of the convoy, the desired spacing. Unfortunately, as with all things Afghan, "time" and "time schedules" are more a concept than a hard and fast rule to be observed. The cordon team arrived to the normal clown festival. No one was sure who was going with whom. The taxis that would be their cover vehicles, hiding their actual affiliation, were nowhere to be found, and there were 10 times more people who wanted to go on the operations than could visibly go without compromising the low-signature intent of the lead element.

The OCI leaders were not satisfied with the believability of two members of the team. As a result, T.T. Boy and Kev were given smelly old robin's egg–blue burqas. They were perfect for the job. The men were starting to look, act, and smell like the Taliban.

When finally they rolled out, they were only minutes ahead of the assault element, and they ended up passing them on the road only 20 minutes into the route. Fortunately, the men knew who it was, and the captain quickly frago'd the plan so the assault element would actually be in front for the first part of the journey.

The convoy passed through the last of Shir Mohammed's checkpoints and set in their ruse. Within eyeshot of the checkpoint, they dismounted and put the 3rd Commandos in place to establish a traffic control point. Any reports on them would tell of another ineffective, static American checkpoint that the Taliban could easily circumvent. In fact, the men would only remain there long enough for the cordon team to pass through, make the northward turn a couple of clicks (kilometers) up the road, and get a 45-minute head start on them.

Then the two taxis pulled up and were stopped. The team guys watched intently as the unwitting 3rd Commandos questioned the driver of the cordon team's taxis. Would the commandos discover their four-man USSF team among the jundis in the cab? The 3rd Commando squad leader stepped back from the window. Satisfied with the driver's story, he waved the two vehicles through. If they could get by the 3rd Commando roadblock, then surely they would travel uninhibited through roadblocks staffed by less motivated and poorly trained Taliban sympathizers.

Time was flying by. Forty-five minutes had passed, and they were rolling down the road. T.T. Boy came up on the SATCOM and gave them a dump of the grid coordinates and number of personnel at each of the checkpoints. "Eight five alpha, this is eight five echo" . . . "Alpha, we're making a pit stop to change drivers, bravo charlie hotel lima hotel echo sierra alpha kilo, we need to top off with three gallons of diesel." "Pit stop" let the captain know that he was talking about a checkpoint at the encoded grid coordinates given by the phonetics, and there were three soldiers with weapons and communications as indicated by the "three gallons of diesel."

Now, this encoded exchange might seem redundant, with SATCOM already encrypted, and the enemy's ability to listen to their transmissions extremely limited. The point was not to confuse the enemy, but to obfuscate the actual meaning of the conversation from hundreds of "friendly" listeners. Since the men were on SATCOM, the whole joint task force was listening. The predetermined code words were critical so they wouldn't tip off headquarters eavesdroppers and radio monitors as to the point of their operation.

The earlier limp-dick memo still hung over the men like a wet blanket. Operations involving real combat had been mandated out from under them, seen as "too risky." CONOP approval was buried in so many layers of command and administration oversight and approval that to "interdict" was out of the question.

If they asked to conduct an operation as a direct action, a raid, or a snatch, the "grammar nazis," as they called them, were likely to microanalyze each syllable, looking for words that didn't please them. A typical long-winded response might be:

"No, no, no, Captain, this just won't do. You cannot say 'sniper-observer.' Instead you must say 'observation post.' Change 'assault element' to 'main effort,' and 'raid' to 'cordon and search.' There, that's better. Now request Predator overflight, AC-130 coverage, QRF standby, TACP support, do an 'ambush assessment' on the route, and once you have all that consolidated and coordinated, come back and resubmit your plan *in two to three days* for further approval." (Make that *dis*approval.)

If approved, it was typically *five days later*; by then, the target was long gone.

The captain found that the only way he could get timely approval was to play by his own rules. They had a growing network of contacts and confidants, but local intelligence tended to be suspect—jundis sometimes lie, believe it or not. Since the captain couldn't be sure that there was even a target, he always wanted to conduct his own "reconnaissance mission." Nothing scared the staff weenies about a recon request.

But, not wanting to risk loose cannons from a SEAL platoon calling in fire on his position, or some stick jockey screaming by overhead mistaking him for a "target of opportunity," the captain would always let them know when and where he was going. He didn't want a 500-pounder dropping on the hood of his Toyota. Of course, the "why" was only for him and his team to know.

As they approached the first checkpoint, Captain Alan yelled through the rear window back to Rock, "Coming up on the first pit stop!" His burley special forces weapons specialist pointed to two of his strikers, and they acknowledged with a nod and a grin. Rock, who barely spoke English, let alone Pashtun, had his own way of communicating with his boys. They would move on his slightest command.

They pulled up to the groggy checkpoint guard, who had an AK-47 slung around his shoulder. He rubbed his eyes and tried to make sense of the looming pickup truck lights. His brain suddenly engaged and he recognized them as Americans. The captain was sure he thought it was an odd hour for a drive-about. Before the guard had time to react, Rock and his two 3rd Commando soldiers were standing next to him.

Through Li'l Kid, who was their interpreter, they exchanged gushing hellos and well-wishes as only Afghans can do: "Hello, how are you? How is your family? How are your friends? Peace be with you, God bless your family . . . ," and so on until the pained look on the guard's face subsided.

"We are American soldiers," the captain told him, "and we are conducting an operation with their Afghan brothers. We are going to secure your weapons and your satellite phone until we come back through here, but these two Afghan soldiers will stay here with you for your protection." With that, Rock's 3rd Commandos removed weapons and communications from the checkpoint, finding out who the checkpoint manning crew worked for. Then the men got back in their vehicles and rolled on down the road, taking down every checkpoint en route, hoping to thwart the early alert network of the Taliban.

Suddenly a voice crackled across the 102: "Beast eight five, beast eight five, this is eight five echo."

"Yeah, eight five. We're stopping to fix a flat tire."

"Roger eight five echo, I copy that you are fixing a flat. Good copy, eight five . . . echo out."

It was good news. They had identified the target compound and were setting their cordon element. There was no distress signal given and no indication that there was a misstep. Beast 85 had covered as many contingencies as possible with encoded verbiage, but none was indicated by the exchange. Red was monitoring the exchange back at Gecko and came up on the 102. "Eight five base copies."

Captain Alan knew he had his finger on the trigger, and was ready to pull. Any indication that they had run into a buzz saw, and Red would immediately alert the QRF commander at Kandahar to get the aircap on alert to provide cover. It gave him a sense of security to know Red was alert to their status even though their radio exchanges would not attract the attention of anyone else.

Beast 85 had entered the town of Sanjin. At 0330 it was a ghost town but for the armed guards that half-slept in front of the shops in the bazaar. They were Taliban, alert to the whoop-whoop of helicopters overhead but not to local Toyota pickups filled with bearded fellows wearing Shawwal kamis. The captain and his men passed through their screen without being noticed. The convoy had tightened up now, interteam communication on short-range FM radios kept everyone in the loop.

"We're about four clicks out."

Captain Alan followed by GPS more intently now. The arrow pointed in a general direction with no correlation to the network of closely lined city streets and alleys. Ringo deftly maneuvered the four-door pickup through the maze, but there was no way of telling which way would punch through to the objective area. They were within a thousand meters of the target, but they couldn't get to it. They started to have flashbacks of *Black Hawk Down*, and they wished they hadn't seen the movie.

"What the fuck, Captain?" Ringo was obviously pissed off. As they would round a corner and stop at a dead end, the line of vehicles would collapse on itself. The inexperienced drivers from 3rd Commando were not disciplined enough to keep their distance, and the compacted convoy would catch hell trying to turn around in the narrow alleyways. Dead ends, an unfordable river, a cornfield—time and time again they pulled the Chinese fire drill maneuver of turning the vehicles within the tight confines of mud-wall-lined roads until they found themselves stopped at a compound wall. The double gates cracked open, and the muzzle of an AK peeked out ahead of the person aiming it. Suddenly there were two, now four, with two appearing at the wall's outer corners.

"Rock?" Captain Alan called back through the split window.

"I've got 'em Captain." Rock had leveled the truck's 7.62 machine gun and peered through its optics at the assembling group of armed men in front of the truck. It was going to get ugly in a hurry, and he was going to scuff them up a bit if they got squirrelly.

"Back the fuck up!" commanded Ringo into the radio as he laid his M4 across his lap and backed the truck up without taking his eyes off the threat to his front. The captain looked back. The trailing vehicles were executing hasty four-point turns and moving back through the alleyway. The growing armed assembly shaded their eyes and squinted into Beast 85's vehicle lights, trying to figure out exactly what was going on. The pickup truck's headlights didn't register as distinctly American, and during their confusion Red and his men were going to get the hell out of there. Ringo backed the truck all the way down the alley, high beams glaring in their faces, barely taking his eyes off the threat to look back. Then Beast 85 was out, back onto the open streets lined with shops.

The captain had to get them into the target area. This wandering around was getting dangerous. He tried to contact the cordon team with the FM. "Eight five echo, this is eight five alpha."

He heard this scratchy reply: "Go ahead, alpha, this is charlie." It was Mike, who they called "Bubble Boy."

"Bubble boy . . . where the hell are you guys? My GPS says we're on top of you, but we can't get there from here."

There was no longer any need for brevity codes since the FM wouldn't carry but a few clicks. "Yeah, Captain, no shit, huh? That imagery is wrong, we are about two clicks past the town . . . where are you?"

They were down along a riverbed, in the area of a lumberyard of sorts, and at 0415 it was starting to get active as people moved about prior to the first call to prayer. Captain Alan slumped into the car seat and covered his face with the turban, hoping they wouldn't notice how pale it was. The cordon team had eyes on the target, but without a good grid to it, Beast 85 would never get there.

Captain Alan asked Bubble Boy to send a contact team back to the town to get them. In the meantime, they spread the vehicles out to provide some security. People were milling about, checking out the 3rd Commando guys in the back of the trucks, and everyone was feeling uneasy. It seemed like an eternity, but in actuality it only took Bubble Boy and his jundi driver about 5 minutes to get to them.

Bubble Boy gave Captain Alan a quick rundown on the target area. It was quite different from how it had been described. The jundis wanted to hit a secondary target, but the special forces guys had contained them. They had already come into contact with a three-man patrol around the mosque, and they had rolled them up. The cordon team was trying to control the area around the target, but they were too small. A rolling assault onto the compound was needed before things got out of hand.

Captain Alan relayed his intent to the special forces guys, and they rumbled down the road and through some back alleys. They would have never found the place without local intel. As they pulled into a dead end, the captain saw Kev, still in his jundi top and turban with desert-camouflage bottoms and boots. He looked ragged. "The OCI guys are a bunch of idiots. We're lucky that they didn't blow the whole thing."

It was daylight now, and Beast 85 was on the bubble. If they lost the initiative, the best-case scenario would be to find nothing. Worst case, they would walk into a buzz saw. It happened very fast. Rock and Flipper grabbed the 3rd Commandos and went running toward the compound. The captain struggled to maintain control of the charged-up assault force. "Drivers! Get these vehicles turned around so we can get out of here in a hurry!"

As Captain Alan made his way down to the compound, the lead jundi came by with the source. It was like something out of a

B movie. The jundi was in his shalwar kamis and sandals, but to conceal his identity, he wore a huge full-faced motorcycle helmet with a dark-gray visor. He was a large man, and he was sweating and dirty. He rambled on incoherently as the captain tried to assess the situation through his interpreter Skippy.

"He says that we're too slow. He says Mullah Osmani will get away, we need to hurry up and get into the house!"

Skippy was trying to be kind, but the captain could tell from his face that the source was bitching. "Tell him to go fuck himself," the captain replied flatly.

"Sir?" (Skippy was looking stressed.)

"I said, he can fuck himself. This is my show, and we are going to conduct this operation according to how we planned it. If he hadn't been so fucked up about the location of the target house, we would have already been in it and gone. He was two kilometers off, and the damn compound looks nothing like what he described."

Skippy tried to play interpreter/peacekeeper as Captain Alan walked away. There was no way he was going to let some jundi get uppity with him and feel like he was in any way important to them.

Captain Alan walked around the corner of a wall and saw the target building. Flipper, Bubble Boy, and Rock were directing 3rd Commando as they took the compound. Homemade ladders were up on the walls and, presto, their sharpshooters were perched atop in overwatch, looking for targets. Snips and home-made halligan tools did the trick and, bam, they were in. They avoided explosive breaching simply because intel can be wrong and jundis sleep all over the place and they didn't want to risk the lives of innocents in a breach.

In front of the mosque entrance, Matt, who they called "Spidey," and a couple of jundis had secured the three guards. Their weapons were separated from them, and they all had that docile "we give up" look that Beast 85 had seen so often. The assault element cleared the compound, and the captain went around to the right-side security position to check out coverage.

Suddenly he heard Kev calling to him. Kev and a 3rd Commando were walking a man back toward the target building. "This guy's a squirter." Kev was referring to the fact that as the assault element breached one side of the compound, the man in custody had fled out the back, and Kev and his 3rd Commando security position had run him down. The captain raced back around to the front of the mosque.

It was the typical postraid chaos. Men were separated and squatted next to an outer wall under guard. Women had been checked by 3rd Commandos to ensure that they were really women under the burqas, not Mullahs, and were contained in a separate guarded room. The compound was secure, and now three-man teams were systematically searching for anything of interest.

"Hey, Captain, look at this!" Ringo presented him with an Afghan identity card and letters from inside the compound. The ID was for Mohammed Akhtar Osmani, and the picture was a slightly heavier version of the man Kev snagged squirting out the back of the compound.

"Hey, Osmani!" Kev held the card up beside the face of the captive and asked again, "Osmani?"

The man looked down without response. Kev and Ringo asked other detainees if they thought the man standing there and the man in the photo ID were the same. None of them responded. They had scared looks on their faces, as if the man was Allah in person. They had all moved away from the squirter when he was brought in. Now they really wanted to get away from him.

"Is that him?" the captain asked the helmeted intelligence asset.

"He says that he is not sure, he thinks so, but Osmani is heavier."

Mullah Osmani had been on the run since November 2001.

"What's your name?" the captain asked the squirter through Skippy.

"Bismallah," came the response.

"Bullshit! You are Mullah Osmani. Ask him again, Skippy."

"Sir, he says that he is just a traveling prophet that came to stay at the mosque."

The squirter was in a loose top, and the captain could see scars from serious wounds on his body. "So where did the prophet get those scars, and why was he in Osmani's house?"

Captain Alan was getting frustrated with this man. They had caught him in Osmani's house, with Osmani's ID, and with mail addressed to "Akhtar Osmani," some of which came from Mullah Omar himself. And now this man expected him to believe that he was just a traveling prophet named Bismallah.

"He says that they are old scars from when he was detained," offered Skippy.

Jake scowled at the captain. "Bismallah translates to 'in the name of Allah.'"

The men didn't have time for Osmani's games, so they rounded up the prisoners, all the paperwork, and loaded the trucks. They had spent far too much time on the objective, and now they were the morning's entertainment for the village. Locals encroached on the gun trucks, and two women wailed and pulled at the garments of two of the five detainees. Some of the local guys waved guns around like they were about to shoot them.

Li'l Kid looked at Captain Alan nervously. "These people are saying bad things, sir. We should get out of here quickly."

The situation was getting tenser by the second, and now there was this new problem. There wasn't enough space in the trucks for all of the detainees and men. Those who had come in by taxi needed a place to sit for the ride home. The 3rd Commandos and the OCI hated each other, so they couldn't be crossloaded into the cars. And to make matters worse, OCI had completely filled one of its vehicles with a nice-looking motorcycle that was in Mullah Osmani's compound.

"Why are they taking that?" the captain asked the OCI leader.

Why bother asking? He already knew the answer. *Prize of war.* He walked away before the OCI leader had even finished with his rambling defense of their actions, and headed back to the detainees. "You and you, get out of here." Then the captain directed Doc to use his shears to cut the zip ties, as Ringo went berserk.

"Why are you letting them go, Captain, just because some whining bitches want you to? What the fuck? That's bullshit."

Captain Alan ignored him. The two men were low-ranking nuggets of minimal value to their efforts, and there just wasn't room for them on the four-hour trip back. Finally they were loaded up and rolling down the street. He was glad that it was over and that he had all his guys in one piece. All they had to do now was get themselves and Mullah Osmani back safely.

They rounded a corner, and out of nowhere appeared a Taliban member wielding an assault rifle. He saw the convoy of vehicles and aimed at it. Suddenly the air erupted with weapons fire. Ringo jerked the truck to a stop as 3rd Commandos started jumping from the truck in hot pursuit. Kev and Bubble Boy tried to stop them and followed them for 30 meters across an open field at the edge of a cornfield into which the armed man had run.

Captain Alan called to them to not pursue. He didn't want them baited into an ambush, and just as they stopped, the weapons fire erupted a second time. Kev and Bubble Boy hit the mud as rounds snapped all around them.

"Cease fire, cease fire!" the captain ran down the line of vehicles trying to rein in the commandos. "Stop firing, we have friendlies to the front."

Once again they got the vehicles loaded and started down the road. This time they made it without event back to the main thoroughfare through Sanjin. As they ran the gauntlet of heavily guarded shops in downtown Sanjin, they passed by the local chief of police and a group of his officers standing at their vehicles. Making sure that he got an eyeful of their catch, the captain gave a courteous, if mocking, wave to the head cop. He saw the moment of realization and fear in the cop's eyes when he recognized their unwilling passenger flex-cuffed in the back of the truck. He knew Osmani was there. He stood speechless and never raised a hand to return the captain's gesture.

The ride back was uneventful. Captain Alan called the firebase and told Red that they were bringing him a present. Red understood immediately. He relayed the word back at the forward operations base that they'd been having some vehicle problems and had stopped in Sanjin. As luck would have it, they had been directed by a local citizen to the home of none other than Mullah Akhtar Mohammed Osmani, where they knocked on the door, detained him, and secured documents that they found. Sheer luck, that was all.

The problem was that "sheer luck" had already led them to a number of weapons caches in the surrounding area, and "sheer luck" during "routine area recon" was starting to sound suspicious to the FOB.

When Captain Alan saw the FOB commander, the commander shook his hand and said with a knowing smile, "Good work, Captain. That was a hell of a route recon.'" He didn't believe any of their bullshit, but there was no bad blood. The end had justified the means.

Mullah Akhtar Mohammed Osmani was detained for two weeks in Bagram, then transferred to an Afghan prison. Several weeks later he was delivered to Quetta, Pakistan, by corrupt local officials for $250,000 in cash. Once in Pakistan, he again took his place as a leader of the Taliban to continue the fight against coalition forces.

So did the end *really* justify the means?

It sure didn't for the source who had given Beast 85 the information. He came and cursed the captain for letting such a dangerous person go after he had risked his family's safety by helping capture him. The team never heard from this source again.

# CHAPTER 14

# TENSE MOMENTS

Beast 85 was now going out several times a week, acting on local intelligence with a few hours' notice, sometimes even mere minutes. They never called them "raids" by name, but rather "route reconnaissance" or "area assessments."

By mid-September 2002, their intelligence network had grown tenfold, and locals were cooperating by the dozens, coming to give the location of this or that cache, this or that radio antenna, this or that Taliban leader or al Qaeda operative.

But it was risky, even downright dangerous, to charge into Taliban territory without proper aerial cover. Beast 85's inform-ants could have played both sides of the game. The men should have fallen into an ambush. They should have been killed. But "do unto the enemy before he does unto you" was their motto. By audaciously taking the battle to the Taliban, they were forc-ing them to fight on their terms, thus multiplying the team's combat effectiveness.

During the third week of August, Beast 85 rounded up and destroyed over 5,000 pounds of explosives and ammunition. The following week, they destroyed another 6,000 pounds, including plenty of AAA and AAA ammo. The forward base seemed to be buying into it, and the team was allowed to conduct more area assessments and route recons.

So they kept "assessing" and "accidentally finding" more and more AK-47s, rockets, antennas, AAA, and SAM missiles. During the last week of August, they rounded up and destroyed more than 11,000 pounds of explosives. The following week, they hit a giant cache where they found 9,000 pounds of ammunition in one shot. The locals had understood the Americans' modus operandi, and they were feeding them with more and more information. The tide had turned. Beast 85 were no longer sitting around like dumbasses in their compound and waiting for the enemy to shell them with rocket-propelled grenades. They were going after al Qaeda and the Taliban, hitting them hard.

The locals started to see Red, Captain Alan, and the rest as victors, and everyone wants to be on the side of the victors. More intelligence came their way. Five days after they'd nabbed Mullah Osmani, their local intelligence friends reported to them that they had some hot, actionable intelligence regarding the hiding place of the third-highest-value target, Mullah Rafiq (a close confidant of Mullah Osmani, Mullah Omar, and Osama bin Laden himself). Among other things, Rafiq was responsible for a brutal ethnic-cleansing campaign directed at the Hazaras. This man had blood aplenty on his hands, not only Hazara but also Turkmen, Tajik, and Pashtun.

Rock, who by now was the team's assault coordinator and liaison to the Afghan 3rd Commando, their personal little army, formulated the actions on the objective. Rock drew out a plan, then created a sand table model of the objective with placards representing the major maneuver elements of the assault troop. Then they war-gamed the sequence of events. What if the compound was heavily guarded? What if they came under fire, and lost one, two, three men, or more?

Beast 85's assault element was made up of 3rd Commando Afghans with their American handlers: Rock, Flipper, and Bubble Boy. They would break down into teams that would put up ladders to provide overwatch or to jump the wall of the compound. They would have someone jump the wall and then open the gate to let the main force in, and carry breaching charges to blow a gate or a wall down, should that be necessary. The Afghans would secure the compound once they were in, and the Beast 85 guys would do the door-by-door takedown of the compound. Once they were inside, a large element outside would seal the objective and keep people from fleeing or attacking.

In the course of 40-plus route recon missions, they nabbed three high-value targets without calling a single helicopter or requesting air cover. In the course of their campaign of accidental findings, they netted over 76,000 pounds of weapons and ammunitions, amounting to over 80 percent of all explosives and weapons found during their stay in the country. There was one team really working in the field, and it was Beast 85.

At one stage, the team had so much to destroy that they arranged for an explosive ordnance disposal unit to send three guys to live with them full-time to help destroy all the ammunition. They also located British surface-to-air "blowpipes" and Chinese surface-to-air HN5s, and they were the team that discovered SA-13s in the country.

Heat-seeking Russian-built SA-13s are among the most advanced surface-to-air missiles, capable of striking a helicopter even at a very short distance. A large, solid Spectre would be toast if one were launched at the aircraft. No one even knew they were in country. Red wanted to take them out the back gate of the firebase to destroy them with the rest of the gear they were blowing up. Instead, after higher-ups got wind of their find, the missiles were sent back to Kandahar Airfield, where the military was sending a special plane to transport the missiles back to the United States for examination. It was a prize find indeed.

Red set up a wall-size white board to track 5-W and CONOP requests. He had time-and-date blocks for each request, listing request status and when approval or rejection was expected. He attached their radio transmission logs to the status board to prevent 5-Ws from being lost in the midst of the FOB, which had been a problem. Red called and asked for the status of the 5-Ws and CONOPS constantly.

The huge administrative burden they were placing on themselves was necessary to keep the FOB on its toes. While no conspiracy theorist, Red prefered to think of the U.S. Army as simply a wasteful, immobile, risk-averse outfit whose purpose is simply to "do time" while minimizing exposure—and political risk to those who run the show.

Maybe a few idiots who somehow ranked as commanders thought grammar and wording were more important than nabbing the enemy.

So there was Beast 85, preparing for its mission to Kandahar, 8 September 2002. The captain was going to sit this one out to get some rest, so Red was going to be the patrol leader. Red had received intelligence that HIG had their leader slip back into Kandahar to organize resistance against coalition forces. The intelligence was collected by the Afghan Office of Civil Intelligence, led by General Gulalai, an ally and a reasonably consistent source of actionable intelligence.

That afternoon, a group of about seven OCI officers and some security guys came by the Gecko compound to go over the details. Beast 85 received their Afghan guests on a veranda of sorts. Their cook made tea and handed out cold sodas as part of the welcoming ritual. They drink a little tea, talk about the weather, the war, and other small talk.

They had learned not to plan these kinds of things in any great detail. Their objectives were never where the Afghans said they would be and looked nothing like they had described them. A detailed plan with a choreographed set of instructions for actions on the objective was a waste of time.

Sure, building plans and compound layouts helped in rehearsing raids and assaults, burning them into memory until they became second nature and you didn't have to think. That was how it worked in a textbook. But in reality, it didn't really work like that. You had to think on your feet—with "think" being the operative word.

Beast 85 was a quick study when it came to adjusting to the realities on the ground. They would rely on standard operating procedures to describe the major moving pieces, then war-game the general scheme of maneuver to getting to the objective. They knew how to assault a compound, even if they had never seen the inside before, so they concentrated on contingency planning: Who would make the initial assault? Who would provide the perimeter security? Who would remain with the vehicles? What would they do if someone were hurt? And what would they do if the entire plan went to shit?

Their flexibility and ability to react quickly to a piece of intelligence allowed them to make a hit with only a few hours of planning. In a pinch, they could roll in less than an hour, even minutes if they had to. By contrast, Task Force 11 required days of planning and tons of Signal Intelligence (SIGINT) and human intelligence (HUMINT) before they would even consider a mission. Task Force 11 did not catch a single high-value target in the months that Beast 85 caught three.

With the OCI guys sipping tea, Beast 85 asked them to describe the compound that the HIG guys were staying in. What was the route to and from the target? What were the obstacles they would have to overcome to get there? What was the expected resistance once they were on the objective? Did they have someone who could walk Beast 85 to the compound? Once they were in, was there someone who could come with them on the objective to identify the bad guys?

They used butcher paper to sketch the compound's layout with the help of the OCIs. This mission would be unique in that it would take place in downtown Kandahar, back in the old part of the city. The vast majority of Beast 85's objectives had been in the villages and towns far away from the city.

The 3rd Commando guys and a few people from the OCI would meet Beast 85 at Gecko at about 2200 hours. They would guide them into the compound, located down an ancient narrow alley through which no car could pass. The plan was to stop the vehicles and drop off the assault teams and the security teams at the entrance to the alley, then move down the alley in stealth. Once they were at the compound, they would put up the ladder teams who were then going to drop into the compound and open the gate. Once the gate was open, Beast 85 would flow into the compound and take it down. They would segregate the persons of interest from the civilians, and then "toss" the buildings, bag the prisoners, and then move back the way they came. If the vehicles came under attack while they were at the objective, Beast 85 would break off the assault and return to the cars to fight. If an attack came from a large force, they would break contact, seal the area, call for reinforcements, and then reassault. It was all pretty straightforward. The plan had enough room to make changes if necessary.

Before dark, T.T. Boy went around to the team's vehicles and did a full check of the communications equipment. He also checked their individual equipment to make sure it was working. Red reviewed the communications plan with him, then they prepped the vehicles, filling them with gas and loading them with ammunition and water.

The kit each guy wore was an individual choice, but they each had some things in common: a bandoleer with about 280 rounds of ammunition loaded in M16 magazines for the M4; a pistol belt with an M9 Beretta 9mm pistol; 60 rounds of ammunition; a trauma pack with dressings and IVs; radio and hand grenades; NVGs; and on their front and back, Kevlar-plated body armor, capable of stopping AK-47 rounds. A few people carried breaching charges to knock holes in walls or open doors, wooden or metal. The Afghans carried rams and sledgehammers to smash open doors. For a quick in-and-out mission like this, everyone carried about 60 to 70 pounds worth of gear. It was heavy stuff.

Red had his kit laid out early that evening. Most kits were assembled and ready to go at all times, so it was only a matter of customizing what you were going to bring rather than digging anything new out of your duffel bag.

The 3rd Commando arrived at 2200 hours. The team briefed them on the mission, going over each action and objective. This was mostly Rock's gig. Flipper and Bubble Boy made sure that Rock didn't go overboard and helped keep things sane.

The six-car convoy pulled out of Gecko at about 0030. Red was in the second SUV along with Ringo and two guys from the OCI. In front of them was an OCI pickup truck with the guide who would lead them to the entrance of the alley. Behind Red's group were two other team vehicles carrying Flipper, Rock, Bubble Boy, Doc Hoss, and Roger. Three pickup trucks filled with 3rd Commando guys pulled up the rear. The entire force consisted of about 20 guys.

They pushed south from Gecko into the city of Kandahar. Kandahar at night is devoid of people on the street. All major intersections have an Afghan army checkpoint, and anyone seen walking around is stopped and arrested. It looked like they were moving through a Hollywood soundstage. The darkness was broken with few electric lights; it was a cityscape straight out of the thirteenth century, without a person in sight. They passed a few checkpoints and were waved through by the soldiers who recognized them.

Kandahar is a small rectangle of a city, with its long axis running east to west. The convoy drove through the south-central old part of the city. The poorly paved road soon gave way to a dirt road, and the lines of shops gave way to irregularly shaped mud walls. Soon, there were very few electric lights to help guide them.

If you drifted off the road and weren't aware of it, you were fucked. So Red lowered his night vision monocular and started to scan the green shapes for any signs of life. The night vision device telescoped into a single Terminator-looking eye. He turned to T.T. Boy in robot-like fashion and started to talk like

Arnold Schwarzenegger. T.T. Boy laughed heartily. Beast 85 enjoyed the dark. Thanks to their night vision goggles, they could stalk in the blackness of night, and the Taliban couldn't.

The convoy turned onto a dead-end road and stopped. The area was lit by a neon-type street light that cast deep shadows around the narrow court. The neon was too bright. Red telescoped the alien-looking night eye upward. The local intelligence guy from the first vehicle pointed toward a dark opening between the 15-foot-tall mud walls that dominated the court. The 3rd Commando guys got into their order of march with the ladder teams up front, with most of the Americans in the middle, and the remainder of the assault team and outside security last.

Red stepped into the alley, lowered his monocular onto his nondominant eye, and scanned the area. The alley was about 8 feet across, with an open sewer running down the middle. On both sides, mud walls of varying heights rose around them. The beginning and end of each compound was possible to discern because of the variations in the walls. They were over 15 feet high. Interspaced along the walls were small wooden doors and gates, the entrances to the compounds beyond the walls.

The assault team moved quickly and quietly along the alley. Red scanned the walls. He and the others were pretty funneled in the narrow alley, and if someone popped up on the wall, Red wanted to see him right away. The alley made a 90-degree turn to the left about a hundred meters in. As he made the turn, he saw the ladder team move into position. They put the ladders up around a small 5- by 3-foot wooden door on the left wall about 25 meters in from the 90-degree turn. Red got on the radio and reported to the security force at the entrance to the alley that the assault team was at the target.

The Afghan team member stood on the top rung and reached as high as he could. The ladder was too short, 5 feet under the top of the wall. Red considered Plan B—maybe they could bring out the ram and smash the door down.

Then Rock moved the ladders back toward the turn in the alley where the wall was much shorter. Red had asked Rock to allow the Afghans to be the first up the ladder or the first in a compound, but there was Rock, first up the ladder, with Flipper and Bubble Boy right behind. As they moved along the wall back toward the compound door, the Afghans followed. They were black shadows. Red was impressed by their light and noise discipline—it was excellent.

Next, Red moved to the door with the rest of the assault element. He gave the brevity code on the radio. They were beginning the assault on the compound. The gate opened with a 3rd Commando guy's smiling face sticking out. It was still quiet, but things were about to change.

The rest of the assault element flowed into the compound just as Rock, Bubble Boy, and Flipper began to take down rooms. Red followed Ringo to a doorway as his number two man and moved into a room. They had bright surefire lights attached to their M4s by a rail on the side of the rifle, so the rifle points where the light shines. There were a kerosene heater, food, various books and documents, and a man and his wife sleeping on a rough mattress on the floor of the room. He sat up as Red and the others walked in. Ringo and Red hit him and his wife with their surefires at the same time, blinding them but refraining from firing.

They told the man through an interpreter to lie on his stomach and put his arms behind him. The woman was speechless at Red's Terminator-like alien eye. Then she started screaming. He had no choice but to throw her out of the room into the courtyard while Ringo flex-cuffed the man on the floor, patted him down, then stood him up to move him out into the courtyard with his wife.

Red gave a quick scan to the surroundings. The entire place was a 20x20-foot square with buildings along all sides of the central courtyard, surrounded by 15-foot walls. Everything was made of adobe.

They hardly had their guy out into the courtyard when Rock and Flipper brought another guy out. Bubble Boy and an Afghan were hauling yet another one out. They had achieved total surprise. Karl von Clausewitz would have been proud.

Before the men left with their prisoners, they needed to do a more detailed search. Meanwhile, things were getting chaotic in the courtyard. The husbands were sitting on their haunches and hurling dark stares at their wives. The women were hysterical. They were running around screaming, pulling their hair, pounding their chests in outrage.

Tensions escalated. Children stood crying on the corner while the women shrieked. Something had to be done. Red told the 3rd Commando boss through the interpreter to corral the women into an empty room and put a guard on the door while they finished up the search.

These prisoners were Pashtuns, and Pashtuns are weird about their women. Females are virtual ghosts in their society. Unless you're related to or married to a female, you never see them. In public they wear dark blue head-to-toe burqas with a narrow mesh opening through which they see the world. To the outsider at least, family is like a prison from which these women cannot escape.

Red asked the 3rd Commando commander to have his men grab the women. This would be better than to have them touched, or even shoved, by the American infidels. Red did this for the safety of the women. Besides, should there be shooting, they could get caught in a crossfire and get themselves killed.

The Afghan commander walked up to one of the women and started to yell at her to move to the room. She was playing a kind of stabbed-sow tragicomedy. The commander started screaming back, and she shrieked even louder. They were getting nowhere.

Rock, Ringo, Bubble Boy, and a crew of Afghans searched the residences within the compound, while Red remained in the courtyard scanning the walls. The shrieking continued.

It was about time to leave. Red heard the 3rd Commando commander's voice rise. He turned and faced him. The commander had not moved a single woman into the rooms as Red had instructed. Instead, he had worked himself into such a huff that he had put the barrel of his AK-47 against the chest of one of the women. Red intervened. He told him forget the women, and get ready to leave.

Elapsed time in the compound: 15 minutes. A lot had happened in a short time.

Red got a head count of the Americans, as the bound men were stood up and shoved toward the door. One of the women clinged to the ankle of her husband as they pushed the prisoners out the small gate into the alley. Red radioed ahead that they were leaving with three guests. They moved quickly, back the way they came.

The vehicles cleared the entrance. As they pulled out of the area, the women came screaming from the alley, waking up the whole city.

By contrast, the drive back to Gecko was uneventful. A military intelligence guy interrogated the three men; one was released and two were taken to Kandahar Airfield for further interrogation, including Mullah Rafiq. A majority of the people who were picked up for questioning were held for a few days and then released, after confiding a few secrets. The team would later hear that Rafiq himself was released, possibly to Khalid Pashtun, political adviser to Governor Shirzai. Ever the opportunist, Pashtun probably ransomed Rafiq to the highest bidder. He was eventually allowed safe crossing into Pakistan, where he continued in exile to advise Taliban operations.

That mission was like so many others Beast 85 had experienced. Sometimes there was gunfire as they approached the targets, sometimes there was a bit of a firefight outside the compound, but because they used stealth, and because the Pashtuns weren't too interested in dying for al Qaeda's cause, they never had to kill anyone during the raids.

Still, these missions were irritating people despite being increasingly successful. One day when Red was at Kandahar Airfield to pick up mail, the battalion's future-plans warrant officer hauled him out of the OPCEN to ask what was going on. He told Red that Beast 85 needed to slow things down.

Laying aside two months of cheating and diplomacy, Red flat-out accused him and the FOB of not wanting to prosecute the war. When the administrative burden got in the way of waging war, then it's time to rethink the administrative burden. The warrant officer looked at Red like he was from Mars, asking him if it was his hope that Beast 85 closed the gates to the firebase and not submit any further mission requests. He said Red's problem was not the administrative burden, but sheer recklessness.

Red told him his (Red's) problem was audacity, sir, not reck-lessness, and his (the warrant officer's) problem, sir, is the absence thereof.

He replied that Red was cheating army procedures and putting the lives of American soldiers in danger.

Red wanted to ask him, "What is your fucking problem?" But he was tired of the bullshit. Instead, he told him that if he thought that he was reckless and was not doing his job, then it was his prerogative to have him removed from his position as Beast 85's team sergeant. He left it at that.

• • •

Of all the contacts Beast 85 made in Kandahar, the Chief of Police General Akram was among the most difficult personalities to figure out. On one hand, he seemed truly interested in better-ing his country. On the other, he was a political animal who would play both sides of the fence. To Captain Alan, Akram's pri-mary interests seemed to be his position and his power base. He'd have done well in American politics.

Akram was also one of the few local leaders who would come to sit down with Beast 85 at their compound. He was con-servative and cautious when providing them with information, but when he did have something to relay, there was a high proba-bility that it was accurate and actionable. When Akram called, he always had the captain's full attention.

Such was the case when he came to visit during the last week of Beast 85's rotation in late September.

A man by the name of Abdul Razaq was a major player in the Taliban. There was some question about his exact title, which var-ied from "Minister of Intelligence in the Helmand Province" to "Deputy Minister of Defense for the Taliban." He was a key player in the assassination of Northern Alliance leader Ahmed Shah Massoud—the "Lion of Panjshir"—and had regular contact with Mullah Omar, Mullah Osmani, and bin Laden himself.

Like many of the Taliban leaders, Razaq simply returned to his familial village after the fall of the regime, where he found protection and had been laying low. According to Akram, Razaq was starting to become active again. He had sent his wife and children away and was ramping up his list of contacts. His goal was to organize mujaheedeen to attack coalition and Afghan Interim Authority targets. He was living in a compound along the Helmand River north of Sanjin, and was being protected by the local police chief.

It was the same scenario Osmani once enjoyed . . . that is, until Beast 85 came a-knocking.

The captain submitted the CONOP, and it was approved—one last opportunity for the gang to run amok. But it was approved with a caveat. The base commander would be coming along on their nighttime patrol.

Captain Alan wasn't exactly thrilled with the idea.

The old commander tried to reassure him. He just wanted a taste of the action. "Look Captain," he said. "I'm not going to take charge or interfere with your operation."

The captain didn't fight it. He knew it would be Beast 85's last patrol regardless, so he didn't have to worry about negative effects on future operations.

After debriefing Akram, planning the patrol, briefing the order, and conducting rehearsals with the guys from 3rd Commando, they were ready to go. The vehicles were lined up, guns mounted, teams kitted, and "angry young man" music turned up to full volume from the captain's truck (this was standard operating procedure throughout the war). But the planned departure time came and went, and they were still sitting there in the dark, revving up, waiting.

Why? The commander had not yet arrived.

"What the fuck, Captain?" Rock exclaimed. "Let's just leave without him." Rock had his commandos loaded up and ready to go. Like the captain, he was getting increasingly irritated by the delay.

It would be a long trip, and they would have to pick up Akram's source en route. The delay risked having to forego Beast 85's "call to prayer," which the captain believed to be imperative for their operation to be successful. In addition, moving a night-time raid into perilous daylight was not high on his list of things to do before he left the country.

Sitting around waiting for hangers-on was tantamount to torture for Beast 85's type-A hostile personalities.

Finally, the commander showed up—an hour late. His excuse was that he had a hard time breaking away from the FOB. Whatever. They had no time to spare in going over the plan, only enough to give him the "*Reader's Digest* condensed" version.

Then, it was time. *"Let's get it on!"* came the war cry from the men.

"About fucking time," Rock grunted with palpable disgust at the commander's tardiness.

When they were about 15 kilometers short of the objective area, the vehicle in which Akram was riding signaled for the convoy to stop. Akram told him through an interpreter that he had to go and get the source in the next village, and that it will take him about 45 minutes.

After six maddening months of operations, the captain had lost his patience with these last-minute surprises. "His guy was supposed to be ready and waiting," he told the terp.

The response from the general was as rambling and incoherent as ever. "He's down the road, now he's up the road, now sleeping, now waiting, now hiding, willing, unwilling, ready, not ready—"

"Tell the general twenty minutes," the Captain interrupted. "Any longer and we are outta here." He was not in the mood for any more bullshit, and he was not going to have his men stuck out in the middle of open Indian country when the sun came up.

The general acknowledged Captain Alan's directive through the interpreter with a nod and pained smile.

It was the Afghan way, to agree with whatever you said, then do whatever the hell they wanted. The captain had seen this before. But further delay threatened to make the timeline and the operation itself a moot point.

Fortunately, Akram was back with his source 15 minutes later. Where had he been? Who knows?—probably drinking tea with the snitch, in no great hurry. The captain didn't really care why, but was grateful the bastard decided to show up.

The remaining team members refreshed themselves on the SOP five-point contingency plan (in case the two-vehicle recon element got hit while pinpointing the objective area). Then Akram's pickup and a team gun truck rolled out to provide security on the leader's recon.

They slipped past the first checkpoint, manned by sleeping guards, and into the village, unnoticed. It was dark, quiet, and bigger than the captain expected. "Gringos" didn't usually come this far north into the Helmand province, so there wasn't much vigilance to speak of, nor did there appear to be any evidence of bad-guy activity, so they kept moving.

But it was not all smooth sailing. When they reached the far end of town, they found a chain barrier stretched across the road.

They could have easily run it down, but stealth was essential to their success. The driver slowed to investigate, and one of Rock's commandos jumped out to remove the barrier. The chain fell, alerting a guard who came running out of a nearby shack. Still groggy from his nap, he jerked the chain back up and into place.

The guard assumed they were trying to get around his unilaterally imposed "tax" on passage. He had a weapon slung on his shoulder, an AK-47. The captain saw the weapon, then saw the look in the guard's eyes change and body stiffen; he had suddenly gained situational awareness. These guys who woke him up were not tax dodgers, but American soldiers.

The guard swung his weapon around by its sling, trying to shoulder it and bring it to bear. His fumbling delay was all that Rock and his commandos needed. Before the Taliban fighter knew what hit him, a commando sent him reeling to the ground with a muzzle to the chest, knocking the air out of him, and pinned him to the ground. The AK landed a few feet away and was secured by another commando. Rock gestured the remaining three commandos into the nearby shack, where they secured the two additional sleeping Taliban shitheads. They were zip-tied and loaded into the truck. They were small time, likely to be questioned and released later, but the risk of having them escape now and alert a larger force was too great.

No shots had been fired, and there was very little yelling, but there was the possibility that Razaq and his Taliban fighters had been tipped. Now the clock was really ticking. The recon was going to have to be abbreviated. Akram's source directed the drivers to an intersection, where one of the roads dead-ended at an irrigation ditch.

"Razaq's house is just through that field, on the other side of the ditches," he said through the interpreter.

"How far?" the captain asked.

The snitch seemed to be struggling with his answer; Afghans are notoriously bad with time and distance.

"How fucking far, Skippy?" the Captain snapped at the interpreter. "We don't have time for this shit."

"Sir, he says not far."

"That's not a fucking answer, Skippy . . . how about this—is it closer or farther than a football field?"

"Football" meant "soccer," and the captain knew how Afghans loved their soccer. He was proud of his quick thinking, coming up with a universally understood unit of measure . . . or so he thought.

"More than a football field," came the vague response.

Shit, that didn't help him. He grew more impatient. "Two, three . . . how damn many?"

"Three, maybe two."

Fine. He could deal with that. It wouldn't help to press the issue more, because the source was only getting more flustered, as was the interpreter.

"Thanks, Skippy," the captain said. "You're doing a great job."

"Thank you, sir," he replied with a pained smile.

The captain returned to the main element and gave the team guys a quick down and dirty. The assault force had readied the ladders and breaching tools. Stretchers were ready, demolition prepped. The boys had been busy for the last forty-five minutes. After a few last-minute questions and clarifications, they were again on the move.

The captain's vehicle slid towards the back of the convoy. He would direct the assault from the rear while the security vehicles remained in place. His men would try to bridge the gap between supporting and assaulting elements. It was not ideal, but hell, he thought, nothing ever went as planned in this damn country anyway.

Now with no sleeping guards or barricades to deal with, they entered the town at full tilt.

Commandos and team guys piled out of the backs of the trucks with their weapons, breaching bags, and two improvised bamboo ladders. As Spidey directed their vehicle into a good position, the captain watched the assault element disappear into the green zone in the direction of the target. After a few minutes, instead of hearing the usual coordinating radio chatter of an assault, he heard the team orienting itself, sounding concerned about navigating the unfamiliar terrain.

On top of that, their inter-team radio signal was getting more and more faint, and the captain realized the compound was further away from the dismount area than 200 to 300 meters. The snitch had guessed wrong.

Captain Alan dismounted the truck. "Spidey, you got this?" he radioed back while he still had a signal. "I gotta get closer to the assault element."

He grabbed a couple of commandos out of two trucks and started toward the green zone. He found himself facing a field of irrigation ditches lined with trees. He radioed to Doc Ken with the assault element. "Where the hell are you guys?"

Doc Ken described the circuitous route of trenches and tree-lined fields they were traveling. Akram's snitch was with them.

Captain Alan worried that the assault would bog down if it had to wait much longer for them to stumble through the dark in search of the compound. "Hey Spidey, get those trucks in position to lay down fire into this green zone if we have to egress in a hurry."

"Got it, Captain."

They were really getting strung out. The captain muscled through the plowed rows of the fields and across plank bridges spanning the series of three-foot-deep irrigation ditches. He was getting more worried by the random radio chatter he was picking up:

". . . taking a piss . . . fits the description . . . where's the source . . . get security . . . hold the assault . . . got the source up. . . ."

From the incoherent message, the captain could not have known what had taken place at the front of the assault: they got Razaq!

Later, he got the whole story from Rock and Spidey. They had entered the green zone with Akram's source and quickly realized that his distance estimation was not even close. They let him out to wander around while the guys leap-frogged security to avoid alerting the enemy and creating a shit-storm. They bumbled about 1,500 meters (a helluva lot more than two or three football fields!) through irrigation ditches and into the lead element of commandos. They were already securing someone with a familiar face, an old guy who looking strangely like Razaq (*but then again*, he couldn't help thinking, *don't they all*).

They needed proof, but their snitch—the one man who could identify Razaq—had gotten tired and lagged behind on the trail. They had already wasted too much time, so the sent a few of the men back to hustle him along.

When he arrived, he instantly smiled and pointed at him. "Razaq!" he announced. His face was smug, and his voice had a "see how good I am" quality. Amazingly, the timing was right according to plan, capturing Razaq only minutes before the first call to prayer. Even the delay through the field was fortuitous, giving Razaq enough time to get up and stumble into a nearby ditch where the commandos rolled up just as he was squatting to relieve himself. They didn't recognize him initially, with nothing unusual about an old Afghan draining the main vein in a field. Still, they were not about to bypass him without checking him out.

Because they were Afghans and not Gringos, Razaq apparently assumed they knew who he was. He tipped his hand, trying to bribe them to let him go; instantly they knew this was someone worth keeping.

At Beast 85's direction, the commandos cleared and exploited the compound, where they discovered weapons, a satellite phone, and a lot of cash, tagging and bagging it for transport to Kandahar Airfield along with Razaq. The team returned to base, where they called it a day. One more shithead rolled up, one less guy to coordinate attacks against U.S., Afghani, and coalition forces.

It was a ridiculous twist of fate, but who were they to question their good fortune. "*Enshalla*," as they say—"As Allah wills it."

But Allah is a funny guy. Just when you think the joke is on the enemy, he turns it back on you. In a bitter case of déja vù, Razaq was released after only a short time in custody—who knows why. Even worse, he would go on to direct at least one known ambush, killing two coalition men. His goal was fulfilled.

Special forces would get the last laugh, though, killing him in a firefight two years later.

*Enshalla.*

• • •

One last opportunity to catch a bad guy practically fell in Beast 85's lap. Red was sitting in the Operations Center at Gecko when the radio came to life. It was Agent Smith of the CIA. He wanted to talk to him right away, so Red jumped on the ATV and rode to his compound.

It was a bombshell: Agent Smith had good, actionable intelligence about where Mullah Omar was hiding!

Mullah Omar was living in different places every few days and traveling with a very small group of bodyguards. The Taliban had learned the hard way that traveling in large convoys with expensive SUVs left a signature that the intelligence people detected. Agent Smith had Mullah Omar living in an isolated valley in northern Helmand province. But access by motor vehicle was impossible. Red called the forward base and asked them to come to talk to Agent Smith at Gecko. They wanted permission from the FOB to start a 24-hour mission planning cycle for an air assault into the valley. There was no point in lying. This was an outright "air assault," not "recon." And there was no way they could "stumble" into the valley.

If the forward base gave them four CH-47s and a few Apache attack helicopters they would pack them with 3rd Commandos and fly up into the valley, performing a classic air assault on the camp. If they met resistance they could back off and let the attack helicopters destroy the place. They could even call in close air support.

Omar would be moving soon, so there was no time to waste.

The future operations officer gave Red the impression he was in agreement. They left and really never said no, but Red waited, and waited, and waited for hours on end as the forward base thought it over. They thought about it until the opportunity passed them by.

The non-decision was a decision in itself, for to drag their feet for 36 hours invited the target to go away. To the captain, Red, and the men of Beast 85, it was a fitting ending to their own great tragicomedy.

So that was that. In an environment where the greatest sin was to fail trying, they did not dare to even try, and Omar moved on to fight another day.

CHAPTER **15**

# RELIEF

B east 85's repeated success with scooping up bad guys had drawn attention, and not all of it positive. The whole "we were conducting an area reconnaissance and got lucky" story had worn thin for the braintrust in Bagram. Somebody decided that they should have a new look at how Beast 85 was doing business.

One day the team received a visit from four soldiers. They were in uniform, clean cut, wearing shiny new gear that hadn't seen a day in the field, and were extremely friendly—too friendly.

"Can I help you?" T.T. Boy asked. He had no problem showing his irritation at interlopers making themselves too comfortable in Beast 85's area. The foursome launched into a song and dance, trying to chat him up. T.T. boy was never particularly chatty anyway, but now these clowns were really pissing him off.

Then they approached Captain Alan. They gave him a rambling explanation of their presence in his compound and why they were talking to his team. They wanted to stay with Beast 85, get a feel for the area, go on few patrols, and on and on. Later the captain would find out from a friend up the chain of command that the foursome was a CID (criminal investigation department) team tasked specifically to come and look into how Beast 85 was getting its actionable information. He was told that they might have been given their task from as high as General Frank's office.

• • •

In mid-September. Beast 85 was invited to send an advance party back to the United States, one guy per team, to set things up for the rest of the guys. Red thought it was important to remain until the entire team had left. The captain surprised him by saying that he wanted Red in the advance party and the hell out of there.

They talked over the decision, and it was obvious that no one on the team was going to hang around Fort Bragg and get things in order for the rest of the group—stuff like getting leave forms filled out, rooms set up, communicating with their wives and girlfriends, getting the team out of harm's way.

So Red went on the roster and was later told that he would be out of Kandahar Airfield within a month and a half.

It was all bullshit. Everybody wanted them out. The guys from 7th SFGA, Beast 85's relief, were already pouring into Kandahar Airfield ahead of schedule. The "summer help" was being replaced. Bullshit, all bullshit.

The 7th Group battalion commander came out to Gecko and looked around. Beast 85 briefed him on the area and what they had accomplished. The commander replied that he was going to put a team at Gecko, a firebase in Spin Buldak, and another in Lash Ga Ghar, with the AOB at Gecko as well. That was a good call. That's what 19th Group had done.

On Red's regular trips back to Kandahar, the 7th Group Battalion was moving into the area full steam. They were the green newcomers, and he was considered the salty old dog. They had that same look of anticipation he had when he had shown up in country six months earlier.

Still, the road they were going to travel would be different from Beast 85's because their special forces group had a completely different culture. Fact was, all the groups are different. The 7th SFGA has a pretty good reputation as a group that is both aggressive and professional. Red wondered if they would be able to really push the envelope and take the war to the bad guys, but then, experience had jaded him.

On 20 September, Red drove to Kandahar Airfield. The weather was getting cool in the evening and the days were not like sitting under a magnifying glass in the sun. It was getting into the 90s during the day. The air was clear. It was a nice day.

Once Red was at Kandahar Airfield, the acting sergeant major told him that the team sergeant from the 7th Group team replacing Beast 85 in Gecko was in town and wanted to meet him. At that moment, it hit him. Red knew he would soon be heading home. The transition out was going to start in earnest. The first advance party from 7th Group was strictly from the battalion staff. The second group was composed of the advance parties from the line companies, which meant that the teams were packing up or were already en route. The FOB had been talking about the rotation back to the States for a couple of weeks. Red went to meet him and ended up giving an impromptu welcome briefing to the entire company leadership. That company was going to take over the southern part of the FOB's AO, which included not only Gecko but a few other places as well.

That week, a few guys from the replacement company stayed with Beast 85 in Gecko. They went on a few missions, set up by Beast 85, and visited Spin Buldak and Lash Ga Ghar. Beast 85 also provided translators, vehicles, and a few guys from the team to accompany them.

It was a great orientation for the replacement crew. They met with local leaders in the greater Kandahar area, learning the complex web of personalities. Red was impressed. They were a long way from their regular AO in South America, but they were good, professional SF soldiers, and they learned fast.

Departure day was originally set for 2 October. But on 27 September the firebase got an urgent radio message: Beast 85 was leaving the next day! Red immediately packed up his little world into two boxes and a rucksack.

Red's belongings were loaded into shipping containers, and he said goodbye to the firebase. Doc Hoss and Rock drove him to the airfield. It felt rather sudden to leave that world behind after six months. Foremost on Red's mind was a tall, frosty glass of beer. He imagined there would be no shortage of that where he was going.

# CHAPTER 16

# HOME

Three days later, Red was back in Germany. He hopped on a C-17 heading to Rhein-Main Air Base. He was glad not to be babysitting any equipment, freeing him up to leave on space-available orders. There were about 20 guys from the FOB on the flight and about 5 from B/3/20. They had an 18-hour layover in Rhein-Main, so they went to the small base pub, still wearing desert camouflage, still dusty, still smelling of Afghanistan.

They got good and drunk. Unlike the rest, Red left the pub early, not wanting to suffer too much on the flight home. He found a nice spot on the terminal floor and proceeded to sleep it off.

The next day they loaded up the C-5. They flew an uneventful flight to Pope Air Force Base, North Carolina, which was surrounded on three sides by Fort Bragg. This was home.

No one was at the airport to meet them. Their sergeant major apparently missed the call that they were coming back. Like any good special forces, they improvised, hitching a ride back to the 3rd SFGA area. One of the rear detachment guys who stayed back at Fort Bragg, Staff Sergeant Rounts, met Red at the 3rd Group area. He handed him a form for a six-day leave and gave him a key to a hotel room in Fayetteville.

Red went to the car impound lot, reconnected his car battery, and drove to the hotel. His wife and kids had gone to a family reunion in Maine, having expected him back in October. Red had called Lorie from Germany and told her that he would fly up to see her. He drove from Fayetteville the next morning to his home in Northern Virginia, stopped by to see his parents, and then jumped on a plane to Portland.

Red and Lorie hadn't told the kids their father was returning. The kids were oblivious as to why Lorie was driving them to the airport in Portland. When they arrived, Red jumped out from behind a column and shouted, "Surprise!"

His three-year-old son didn't know who he was, and his six-year-old daughter looked up at him and then down at her shoes. She seemed terrified. It was too much for her to take. But a few minutes later the shock had subsided, and they were all together again as if Red had never left.

Red's leave was to be short, and he had to return to Fort Bragg to get the rest of the team back, cleaned up, and out on leave. As they returned in three big groups, he made sure that nothing was really expected of the guys. He handed them leave forms and hotel keys. They could go away for a few extra days as long as they called periodically to check in with him.

Once leave ended, the men were back in the same place they were when first activated. Third Group threw the B-team out of their office the second day they were back and cut Beast 85 loose with a group order. Red and the others returned and went straight to the MODRE, or mobilization and deployment readiness exercise.

The MODRE was still run by the same idiots as before. They had to go through the same records review, the same physicals, the same day-in-day-out mind-numbing bullshit. They had to get through it to get off of active duty and go home.

It took two full weeks for the men to get out of the MODRE. They got physicals, cleaned and inventoried all of their gear, and got their personal folders together. It was slow, monotonous work. They had four-day weekends every week, and drove home every chance they got.

Just before the MODRE released them from active duty, they had a formation with some VIPs as part of the "goodbye ritual." Brigadier General Vincent Brooks told them they had done a great job. Red asked him if he truly meant it. "Yes," he said, "and we've learned a lot through you guys."

It turned out Beast 85 had been a test company to see if the National Guard special forces groups were up to the task of deploying into combat and being successful. General Brooks thought they were, but he did say that "procedural problems did arise." What an understatement!

They loaded all their gear into shipping containers and onto flatbed trucks for transport back to their old unit. Next stop was Fort A. P. Hill, back to where it all started. They were done.

# RED'S POSTSCRIPT

On 5 January 2004, the *Washington Times* ran an article that stated that the army missed capturing Mohammed Omar once more because the special forces team currently at Firebase Gecko, which had received the intelligence about his location, was denied permission to go after him. Instead, the word was relayed up the chain of command, then back down to Task Force 11. By the time they got to the spot, Omar was long gone.

The debate keeps raging in the highest ranks of our government and military over the best way to conduct the war on terror. The easy, and most supported way right now, is the direct-action approach: kicking down doors. But the easy way isn't necessarily the best way. Hunter-killer teams are only effective if we know where the enemy is. And electronic intelligence can only pick up so much information, as the continued freedom of Osama bin Laden and Mullah Omar indicate. Such tactics will only breed more ill will in places of the world where Americans are already hated.

The idea of winning the hearts and minds still has a bad ring from the Vietnam era, but it must be remembered that the Vietnam War had a very different goal from the war on terror. As Beast 85's story shows, the people who have the boots on the ground are the ones who have the best chance of knowing what is really going on and of taking action.

In the *Washington Post* article, the writer quotes scholars of military theory: "They might be experts at some level, but have they ever had a weapon in hand?"

The Bush administration, though, is listening to these "experts" and moving away from the traditional special forces counterinsurgency missions to focus on door-kicking missions. Such a path fails to even see how the greatest coup in the past two years was the capture of Saddam Hussein. It was by working with locals that the army was able to find his hole and capture him. Hearts and minds must be won, and special forces are the primary units to accomplish that task.

• • •

From the second I arrived at Fort Bragg, I sensed an organizational bias against the National Guard. We call it a "different shade of green." We were immediately relegated to support roles and staff tasking. The army has created a huge command structure that destroys any ability to act quickly or decisively. Commanders simply do not trust the leaders on the ground to make the decisions they're supposed to make. I heard with my own ears to just sit still and finish my tour of duty. But Beast 85 would not sit still and finish its tour of duty without nabbing Taliban leaders and al Qaeda operatives. Beast 85 would talk back and argue. Beast 85 was questioning and rebellious because our men were better educated, had more military experience, and had years of law enforcement experience.

What really made Beast 85 so successful was our ability to think outside the box, to focus on the mission, and to aggressively pursue the enemy regardless of the obstacles, including the insane administrative burdens placed on us by our own headquarters.

The U.S. Army Special Forces is one of the most overdeployed, underutilized units in the army. The original 5th Group teams (the famous 300 horse-riding special forces warriors) had conquered the entire country back in late 2001 because their teams were encouraged to do whatever it took. They operated independently without much direct supervision on some of the hardest terrain on earth and accomplished the mission. Their feats are now the stuff of legend. Was it because they were any different from most SF A-teams? No, it was because they were allowed to do their job as they were trained. They were given a mission, and they accomplished it by being able to adjust quickly and decisively to the tactical situation on the ground without interference from the higher headquarters.

Once the CJSOTF and CTF180 were established in Afghanistan, the special forces battalions became, in effect, conventional troops. The command overhead became so huge that it diminished our ability to accomplish our mission. It was unnecessary, and indeed counterproductive, to set up an entire CJSOTF with only two battalions of special forces in the field, and it was an even greater mistake to place the CJSOTF under a conventional task force commander. It was unnecessary to make the task force commander a three-star general when he was commanding such a small force.

For all the bickering and unpleasantness, the men of Beast 85 answered their country's call when it came, said goodbye to their comfortable lives back home, and willingly went into harm's way, not because they love war, but because they love one another, and they love the United States of America.

# LIST OF ABBREVIATIONS

| | |
|---|---|
| 11B | infantry MOS |
| 18A | Special Forces Officer Carrier Branch |
| 18B | Special Forces Weapons MOS |
| 18C | Special Forces Engineering MOS |
| 18D | Special Forces Medical MOS |
| 18E | Special Forces Communications MOS |
| 18F | Special Forces Intelligence MOS |
| 18Z | Senior Special Forces Sergeant MOS |
| AAA | antiaircraft artillery (fire) |
| AAR | after-action review |
| a/c | aircraft |
| ALT | alternate |
| ALZ | alternate landing zone |
| AMF | Afghan military force |
| AO | area of operations |
| AOB | advanced operations base (usually a special forces company staff) |
| AQ | al Qaeda |
| AST | area specialty team, or administrative guys |
| CAG | combat action group (DELTA Force) |
| CAS | close air support |
| CID | criminal investigation unit |
| CJSOTF | Combined Joint Special Operations Task Force— |

|  | in charge of all U.S. and coalition special operation forces in a theater of operations |
|---|---|
| CJTF | combined joint task force |
| CONOP | continuous operation, an addition to a larger operations order |
| e-CAS | emergency close air support |
| EALT | earliest anticipated launch time |
| EIO | electronic intelligence officer |
| EPA | evasion plan of action |
| FLIR | forward-looking infrared system |
| FOB | forward operating base—usually a Special Forces Battalion Staff |
| FRAGO | fragmentary order (*also* FRAGORD) |
| GPR | ground positioning receiver |
| HLZ | helicopter landing zone |
| JDAM | joint direct attack munition |
| LMTV | light medium tactical vehicle (replaces 2 1/2-ton truck) |
| LZ | landing zone |
| MODRE | mobilization and deployment readiness exercise |
| MOS | military occupational specialty |
| MSS | mission support site |
| NCOER | noncommissioned officer evaluation report |
| NLT | not later than |
| NORSOF | Norwegian special operations forces |
| NVG | night vision goggles |
| ODA | Operational Detachment Alpha—the 12-man A-team |
| ODB | Operational Detachment Bravo—the B-team, or company staff |

| | |
|---|---|
| ODC | Operational Detachment Charlie—the C-team, or battalion staff |
| OER | officer evaluation report |
| OPCEN | operations center; a war room with maps on the wall and radios all over the place |
| OPCON | operational control |
| PAX | passengers |
| PLZ | priority landing zone |
| PRI | priority |
| PUC | person under suspicion |
| QR | quick reaction |
| QRF | quick reaction force |
| ROE | rules of engagement |
| SATCOM | satellite communications |
| SFGA | Special Forces Group (Airborne) |
| SIGINT | signal intelligence |
| SITREP | situation report |
| SOF | special operations forces |
| SOP | standard operating procedures |
| TACP | tactical air control party (Air Force) |
| TF | task force, made up of several units |

# SPECIAL FORCES BASICS

The term *special forces* is often confused with the term *special operations*. Special forces consists of a specific group of units within the U.S. Army known as Green Berets. Special operations consists of many different units. U.S. Army Special Forces, Rangers, Navy SEALs, and DELTA Force are all part of the special operations community.

The U.S. Army Special Forces is made up of the 1st, 3rd, 5th, 7th, and 10th Special Forces Groups in the regular army. These groups are all geographically aligned with certain areas of the world. The Army Reserve has the 19th and 20th Special Forces Groups.

Each special forces group is divided into four battalions. Three of the four battalions are line battalions with operational companies; the fourth is a support battalion. Each of the line battalions has four companies, three operational companies, and a battalion headquarters company. Each line company has five special forces A-teams, the operational element in the special forces. The A-team is where the meat hits the metal.

While the First Special Service Force might officially be the grandfather of modern special forces, in reality, most Green Berets look back toward another World War II force—the OSS, Office of Strategic Services, founded by Colonel "Wild Bill"

Donovan. The OSS was patterned after the British SOE—Special Operations Executive. The OSS was designed to operate behind enemy lines in small groups, primarily by linking up with partisan groups, particularly the French Resistance.

In the Pacific theater, guerrilla units formed by men who disappeared into the jungle after the Philippines were overrun by the Japanese formed the basis of covert units there. Colonel Russell Volckmann is credited with helping to organize much of the resistance in the Philippines and for developing much of the guerrilla warfare doctrine of the U.S. Special Forces

When Red arrived in the 2nd Battalion, 10th Special Forces Group (Airborne), his battalion commander gave him the book *Bodyguard of Lies* to read. One story about the OSS that made a strong impression on him was about a Jedburgh Team that was sent into a French Resistance network that the Allied commanders knew had been compromised and taken over by the Gestapo.

Prior to departing, the team was given a briefing containing false information, believing, of course, it was true. When they parachuted in they were immediately picked up by the Gestapo, tortured, and eventually gave up this information, which the Germans likewise believed to be true. It didn't occur to the Germans that the English and American men who ran the SOE and OSS would deliberately sacrifice a team of their own people like this. But as Churchill said, "Sometimes the truth must be protected by a bodyguard of lies."

In 1952, Colonel Aaron Banks, a former OSS operative, convinced the army to form special forces to exploit resistance potential in Eastern Europe. This unit was to be based on lessons learned in France, the Philippines, Burma, and other theaters of operations. Thus in 1952, the first special forces unit consisting of a grand total of 10 men was formed on Smoke Bomb Hill at Fort Bragg, North Carolina.

Many of the early members were men from those countries who joined the American army as a way to gain citizenship and also in the hope of one day freeing their home countries. The special forces motto, *De Oppresso Liber* (Free the Oppressed) came from these early days of the Cold War.

Among the first Americans in Vietnam were special forces advisers. They were there to train indigenous forces in counter-insurgency, the opposite of what they had been preparing for in the 10th Special Forces Group. In 1961, President John F. Kennedy visited Fort Bragg and inspected the famed 82nd Airborne Division and the special forces. Kennedy soon sent a letter to the army indicating his support for the previously unauthorized green beret, saying it was a "symbol of excellence, a badge of courage, a mark of distinction in the fight for freedom." Today the terms *Green Beret* and *special forces* have become interchangeable. Two other distinctive emblems of special forces are the patch and the crest.

 The arrowhead shape of the patch represents the craft and stealth of Native Americans, America's first warriors. The upturned dagger represents unconventional warfare missions. The three lightning bolts represent blinding speed and the three methods of infiltration—air, land, and sea. The gold represents constancy and inspiration, and the teal blue represents all the branch assignments from which special forces are drawn.

On the crest, the crossed arrows again refer to Native Americans and the original unconventional warriors on the continent. The fighting knife represents the character of the special operations soldier: straight and true. Along the base is the motto of special forces.

One misconception about special forces is that they are cold-blooded killers and snake-eaters. In reality, their primary mission is to teach others in areas that run the spectrum from combat operations to civil engineering to medical training.

Special operations forces, then, include all elite units from the military services consisting primarily of the following:

## UNITED STATES ARMY

### Rangers

The 75th Ranger Regiment consists of three battalions of approximately 800 men each. This is the army's elite light-infantry strike force.

### Task Force 160, Special Operations Aviation Brigade

Also known as the Night Stalkers, it includes two battalions of helicopters. They fly three types of choppers, all modified for special operations: the MH-60 Night Hawk, a modified Black Hawk helicopter; the MH-53, a larger type of helicopter primarily used for carrying troops and supplies; and the MH-6 Little Bird, which can be used as a gunship and to carry a small number of men.

### DELTA *Force*

Once part of the army, DELTA Force now reports directly to the Department of Defense. The assault on Mullah Omar's compound was planned and approved by DoD chief Donald Rumsfeld.

## UNITED STATES NAVY

### *SEALs*

SEAL stands for Sea, Air, Land. They are technically responsible for operations in water and up to the high-water mark. There are two SEAL Naval Special Warfare Groups (NSWG), one at Coronado, California, and the other at Little Creek, Virginia. SEAL Team Six is the navy's elite counterterrorist team.

## UNITED STATES AIR FORCE

### *The 1st Special Operations Wing, SOW*

The SOW flies the following:

MC-130 Combat Talon, which is a modified C-130 Hercules transport with all-weather capability and Fulton Recovery system. Flies low to the ground to infiltrate enemy territory.

HH-53 Pave Low Helicopter: a modified CH-53 Jolly Green Giant with all-weather, all-terrain capability. This was designed to address the failure at Desert One.

AC-130 Spectre Gunship: a modified C-130 Hercules transport designed to be an airborne gun platform with a 105mm howitzer, 40mm Bofors cannon, and two 20mm cannons.

## UNITED STATES MARINE CORPS

The marines technically don't have a special operations unit. The entire corps is considered a "special operations capable" force.

Inside U.S. Army Special Forces are five active-duty special forces groups, each consisting of three line battalions with three companies in each with five A-teams in each company:

1st Group is headquartered in Fort Lewis, Washington, with one battalion forward-deployed on Okinawa. It is responsible for the Far East.

3rd Group is headquartered at Fort Bragg, North Carolina. It is responsible for the Caribbean and Africa.

5th Group is headquartered at Fort Campbell, Kentucky. It is responsible for the Middle East and southwest Asia.

7th Group is headquartered at Fort Bragg, North Carolina. It is responsible for Central and South America.

10th Group is headquartered at Fort Carson, Colorado. It is responsible for Europe and has one battalion forward-deployed near Stuttgart, Germany.

**A-TEAMS**

The A-team is the operational element of special forces. It is designed to conduct operations completely on its own, unlike the rest of the army, which has a hierarchy of tactical and strategic operations. The term *A-team* is taken from Operational Detachment Alpha, or ODA. Its higher command is a B-team, Operational Detachment Bravo, or ODB. This is the equivalent of a company. There are five A-teams per B-team. Above that is the C-Team, Operational Detachment Charlie, or ODC. This is the equivalent of a battalion.

An A-team consists of 12 men as follows:

**Team leader**: a captain who exercises command of the detachment and can command/advise an indigenous combat force up to the battalion level. Note that this is in alignment with the special forces' primary mission of being a force multiplier. An A-team is capable of recruiting, organizing, training, and fielding a battalion of indigenous troops, or about 200 soldiers.

**Team sergeant**: Officially known as the Operations Sergeant, he is the senior enlisted member of the detachment. He advises the team leader on operations and training matters. He provides tactical and technical guidance and professional support to detachment members. He prepares the operations and training portions of area studies, briefbacks, and operation plans. He can recruit, organize, train, and supervise indigenous forces up to battalion size.

**Executive officer**: Officially known as the detachment technician, this man serves as second-in-command and ensures that the detachment commander's decisions and concepts are implemented. He prepares the administrative and logistical portions of area studies, briefbacks, and operation plans. This position is filled by a warrant officer.

**The assistant operations and intelligence sergeant** plans, coordinates, and directs the detachment's intelligence collection, analysis, production, and dissemination. He also assists the Operations Sergeant and replaces him when needed.

**Two weapons sergeants** employ conventional and UW tactics as tactical mission leaders. They train detachment members and indigenous personnel in the use of individual small arms, light crew-served weapons, and antiair and antiarmor weapons. They recruit, organize, train, and advise or command indigenous combat forces up to company size.

**Two engineer sergeants** supervise, lead, plan, perform, and instruct all aspects of combat engineering and light-construction engineering. They construct and employ improvised munitions; plan and perform sabotage operations; and recruit, organize, train, and advise or command indigenous combat forces up to company size.

**Two medical sergeants** provide emergency, routine, and long-term medical care for detachment members and associated allied or indigenous personnel. They establish medical facilities to support detachment operations. They recruit, organize, train, and advise or command indigenous combat forces up to company size.

**Two communications sergeants** install, operate, and maintain FM, AM, HF, VHF, UHF, and SHF radio communications in voice, CW, and burst radio nets. They recruit, organize, train, and advise or command indigenous combat forces up to company size.

The A-team is designed to be even more of a force multiplier when operating in split-team mode, with one of each specialty on the two six-man teams.

### Special Forces Missions

A special forces team is tasked with planning and conducting the following missions:

Direct action: conduct operations such as raids, ambushes, and demolitions

Reconnaissance: serve as the eyes and ears, usually at a strategic level

Unconventional warfare: support the guerrillas

Foreign internal defense: support a government against the guerrillas

Infiltrate and exfiltrate by air, sea, and land: get in and out of any place in the world

Conduct remote operations with little support

Train indigenous forces

Of all special forces schools, Medic is the toughest. Military Occupational Specialty (MOS) 18D is notorious for never being filled due to the duration and difficulty of the course. Each detachment member has an 18-series MOS, which means that they've attended and graduated the special forces qualification course.

The course is divided into common tasks and then MOS-specific tasks. The course lasts from six months to a year depending on the MOS. Medic (18D) is the longest, and Weapons (18B) is the shortest. Entire teams are then divided into several specialties. Lately there has been an emphasis on teams picking a reconnaissance or DA (direct-action) emphasis. Recon teams watch the enemy, DA teams assault them.

Red is a member of Bravo Company, 3rd Battalion, 20th Special Forces Group. He is the Operations Sergeant of Special Forces Operational Detachment Alpha (SFODA) 2085, or Beast 85. The 5 in 2085 means that it's a SCUBA team. Beast 85 is a DA (direct-action) team, through and through.

# WHAT ARE THEY DOING NOW?

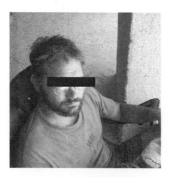

**Bubble Boy** is a lieutenant in a fire department.

**Doc Hoss** is a teacher for a special forces medical course.

**Doc Ken** is a fireman.

**Flipper** is a consultant for military contracting organization.

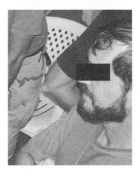

**Kev** is a government contractor in military modeling and simulation.

**(L to R) Rock** is a SWAT team member and works in military contracting.

**Ringo** is a SWAT team member.

**Mongo** works for the Army National Guard.

**Spidey** is a college student and runs a professional landscaping business.

**Stitch** is a range control officer.

Beast 85's good friend and comrade in arms **T.T. Boy** died tragically after returning from Afghanistan. He is survived by his wife Carla and young son Cole.

**"RED" (ADAM)** is operations sergeant of a Special Forces Operational Detachment Alpha (A-team) known as Beast 85. He attended the Special Operations Course in 1983, then served with 5th Special Forces Group before going to college and enlisting in the National Guard. As a Guardsman, he was mobilized in 1991 for Desert Storm. After the war, he joined the Department of State, working at several embassies in Latin America and the Far East, followed by graduate school. After graduating, Adam began a new career in information technology. Prior to 9/11, Adam was promoted to master sergeant and appointed as the noncommissioned officer in charge of an A-team before the team was sent to Afghanistan. Since returning from Afghanistan, Adam has continued his work as an IT expert.

**"CAPTAIN ALAN"** was the detachment commander of Beast 85 during operations in Afghanistan. Originally an enlisted soldier, after graduating from college he was commissioned as an infantry lieutenant. He then served as infantry platoon leader and infantry company executive officer before being selected for and completing the Special Forces Officer Qualification Course. Following his deployment to Afghanistan in 2002, Captain Alan left active military duty while continuing to work as a civilian for the Department of Defense. He continues in the National Guard and was recently promoted to major and assumed command of a reserve component special forces company.